"Alexandra has written a groundbreaking book of spiritual and practical wisdom that explores new uses of the imagination in healing loss. If you ever thought it was too late to express love or to forgive someone, try the exercises in this book! This big-hearted book is a gift to us all."

—Gerald G. Jampolsky, M.D., author of *Forgiveness: The Greatest Healer of All*

"Enormously helpful . . . the author gives us the practical means to free ourselves from life-inhibiting emotions. Beautifully written, and highly recommended for those still battling unresolved grief."

—Kenneth Ring, Ph.D., author of *Lessons from the Light* and *Mindsight*

"Refreshingly original in its approach, *The Infinite Thread* takes loss beyond conventional ideas of mourning. The insightful series of exercises and thoughtful text make this book essential reading for all those who seek healing and resolution in their grief."

—Charles Garfield, author of *Sometimes My Heart Goes Numb*

"To experience loss is a fact of life. Yet so many of us simply shut out what causes pain only to learn over time that this shutting out robs us of our very lives. This book offers a path to healing from the inside out . . . a way not only to comfort but to the joy of regaining our own lives."

—Hal Zina Bennett, author of *Write from the Heart*

"Alexandra Kennedy makes safe the rite of passage we all would give anything to avoid: into death and grief. . . . Yet Kennedy compassionately guides the way to inner healing with truth, comfort, and even joy by restoring faith that love is eternal and that we are always connected."

—Beth Witrogen McLeod, author of
Caregiving: The Spiritual Journey of Love, Loss and Renewal

"In *The Infinite Thread*, Alexandra Kennedy gives us tangible tools and ways to reconcile a relationship with a loved one and to work through unfinished business. . . . This book is an excellent resource guide for healing all our relationships."

—Angeles Arrien, author of *The Four-Fold Way* and *Signs of Life*

The Infinite Thread

The Infinite Thread

Healing Relationships beyond Loss

Alexandra Kennedy

BEYOND
WORDS
Publishing
I N C

Beyond Words Publishing, Inc.
20827 N.W. Cornell Road, Suite 500
Hillsboro, Oregon 97124-9808
503-531-8700
1-800-284-9673

Editor: Hal Zina Bennett
Managing editor: Julie Steigerwaldt
Proofreader: Marvin Moore
Design: Principia Graphica
Composition: William H. Brunson Typography Services

Printed in the United States of America
Distributed to the book trade by Publishers Group West

Library of Congress Cataloging-in-Publication Data
Kennedy, Alexandra.
    The infinite thread : healing relationships beyond loss / Alexandra Kennedy.
        p.   cm.
    Includes bibliographical references.
    ISBN 1-58270-046-X (pbk.)
    1. Grief.   2. Bereavement—Psychological aspects.   3. Death—Psychological aspects.   4. Loss (Psychology)   I. Title.
BF575.G7.K458   2001
155.9'37—dc21

                                                        00.068077

The corporate mission of Beyond Words Publishing, Inc.:
Inspire to Integrity

For Jon

Contents

Foreword

It is unbelievable that a moment will come when each of us must die. Death is the loneliest event in life. Forced expulsion into the absolute unknown, to leave everything familiar. No one can go with you. Once you leave, you cannot get back. No one knows where you have gone. You can send back no message. Give no sign. No one will ever see your face again.

Death is the most terrifying prospect. It is one of the incredible achievements of humans to be able to forget how death hangs over us. Postmodern consumerist culture has banished death. Its relentless distractions prevent the mind focusing on death. Even when it allows death to surface, it is neutralized in bland image and fake words.

Yet somewhere within, each of us remembers. We glimpse the figure of Death through the crevices of our fragile shelter. We know Death will come. It always knows where we live. Consequently, something within us realizes that the conversation with our death cannot be put off indefinitely. The irony is, of course, that as soon as we begin this conversation, we discover that death is not a crude monster of annihilation. Death reveals itself as the secret well where eternity flows toward us and with us. The conversation with Death is the beginning of the transfiguration of fear and negativity. Sometimes this conversation only begins and becomes real when we lose someone we love. This is the beauty and subtlety of Alexandra Kennedy's book.

Alexandra Kennedy engages the threshold of dying and death with such sure gentleness. The lyrical subtlety of her writing veils the grain and grit of its truth. She offers mythology, narrative, and empirical data as pathways to the embrace of the dying and the retrieval of grief not as a desert but as a slow garden of remembrance, surprise, and unexpected novelty. The book is a practical tool and will be immensely helpful to so many wounded ones forsaken at a frightening threshold. Rich in imagination, it invites us to let our imaginations become pathways to retrieve subtle presences hidden under surface absence.

John O'Donohue

Acknowledgments

I especially want to acknowledge my agent and editor, Hal Bennett, who took this book (and my first one, *Losing a Parent*) under his steady wing, provided wise guidance, and found just the right publisher; Cynthia Black, Richard Cohn, and the staff at Beyond Words Publishing for giving this book so much tender loving care; and poet John O'Donohue for the gift of his foreword. Its powerful message and exquisite use of language brings me to my knees in admiration. Special thanks to Barbara Connor for being so gently persistent and caring in the delivery of the foreword.

My profound thanks to my students at the Institute of Transpersonal Psychology, whose contributions have greatly enriched this book, and to Robert Frager for bringing me into the ITP family; to my clients who inspired me with their courage in the face of grief; and to all those who shared their stories in workshops, letters, and interviews. Your sharing has blessed my life and will, I hope, bless the lives of many others. To honor confidentiality, I have changed names and identifying details, except when requested to do otherwise.

To my friends who offered love, moral support, and fresh ideas—thank you! I wish I had space to name you all, but I hold every one of you in my heart in gratitude. My thanks also to my dream group for weekly infusions of spirit. To Patty Flowers at University of California Extension, I offer my loving gratitude for her friendship and belief in me—and for offering my first class on this subject. I deeply appreciate Beth Witrogen McLeod's enthusiastic support of my work over the past ten years; her heartfelt book on caregiving is helping so many people. To my teachers, especially Stephen Levine, James Hillman, and Kenneth Ring, whose teachings on dying, grieving, and imagination have had a profound impact on my work—and this book. I am eternally grateful that Creation brought Joy Clift into my life at this stage of my journey; her laughter and love permeate every cell of my being.

I feel grateful beyond measure to my family for their enduring love and generosity, especially my mother, Dan, Van and Beth, Bob and Dawn— as well as my father, who has been a nurturing presence within me. My son deserves special thanks for his contribution of hugs, passionate drumming, and adolescent perspective. I am truly blessed that this heartful and talented young man is my son. My husband, Jon, once again has been my toughest critic and greatest support. His love, intelligence, and guidance permeate this book and every aspect of my life. After over thirty years of marriage he is—more than ever—the love of my life. This book is dedicated to him.

Introduction

The intensity and power of my grief in the first year after my father's passing humbled and frightened me. Even with my experience as a psychotherapist, I was not prepared for the waves of feelings that arose from my depths and bowled me over. I was not prepared for the excruciating sense of aloneness, for the sobering sense of my own mortality, for the changes in my relationships. His death impacted every aspect of my life—it rearranged my insides, broke down old structures, churned up unresolved issues, and brought everything into question.

Grief, like childbirth, activated primal forces that surged through me in waves, filling me with anguish, longing, relief, anger, depression, numbness, despair, guilt, and often unbearable pain. I was caught up in a momentum that I could not slow down or stop. These forces were not rational, reasonable, predictable; I was frightened to feel so out of control. In the shadow of birth and of death, I was in touch with powers greater than me—an experience that humbled and humanized me.

We so often get in the way of grief; we try to suppress, truncate, postpone, or ignore it. We are afraid of being overwhelmed, of becoming nonfunctional: "If I start crying, I'll never stop." Many of us resist grieving because we think that what we are experiencing is abnormal. We are also afraid that our friends will feel uncomfortable and withdraw from us. Since we live in a culture that expects quick fixes and avoids pain, there is a tendency to pull oneself out of grief prematurely. There can in fact be considerable pressure from friends and family to "pull yourself together and get on with your life."

But grief is more powerful than our resistance. In grief, it is natural, though uncomfortable, to feel raw, vulnerable, alone, overwhelmed. Even if we manage to suppress it, we compromise our living. We have to shut down. We can't afford to be near anything that might trigger it. Unresolved grief shows up in our lives in symptoms such as chronic physical problems, depression, addictions, and compulsive behavior. And at some later time, often when it is least expected, the grief erupts.

How can we surrender to the tides of grief? How can we deepen into it without feeling overwhelmed? How can we heal our regrets? I often recommend that people who are grieving create a sanctuary, a sacred place where you can sit each day with your grief. I encourage you to use this time to explore the intense feelings and thoughts aroused in grief— you can write, cry, sing, meditate, pray, or just sit. It is helpful to set up an altar there with pictures, special objects, candles, flowers. This sanctuary is the place where, in the midst of our busy lives, we can honor our grief. It is the place where we can deepen into our grief and let it work on us. Each time we use our sanctuary, we get the nourishment and strength to go further in the process. As time goes on, we may need to use the sanctuary less frequently, but we can still use it to check in with ourselves.

If you wonder whether you are avoiding or suppressing your grief, I suggest that you use your sanctuary for at least fifteen minutes a day— to spend that time to listen, slow down, check in. If you are feeling good and nothing much is coming up, that's fine, but keep checking in. This way you are honest with yourself about your grief.

I see the sanctuary as a central strategy for grieving fully without feeling overwhelmed. It is important to spend time alone with oneself. Sharing one's grief with others is also important. Many people feel isolated and even ostracized in their grief, and it is a great relief and comfort to be with others who are having the same kinds of experiences.

On the twelfth anniversary of my father's death, I led an all-day "After Loss" workshop. In the morning, each participant briefly shared his/her story, words mixed with tears and at times deep sobbing. The woman on my right had lost her six-year-old daughter two years before.

The woman on my left had lost her brother to the military death squads in Honduras; his body had never been found. The adult sons of two of the women had committed suicide. Another mother was grieving the death of her adult daughter to a sudden illness. Many of the participants had lost parents; others, husbands. Inside that room there was so much grief that at times we felt our collective heart would break. Each loss was our loss; each grief embraced and shared. Most of these people had not talked so freely with others about their grief. When it was a young woman's turn to speak, she told us that her friends insist she has been grieving too long. "They don't know what I'm going through at all. I just want to know that I'm OK, that I'm not crazy to be grieving like this." She was asking for the support and encouragement we all need.

Included in our circle were the photographs of our deceased loved ones, their faces brimming with the life that had now left them. My father's picture was there. He was leaning against the railing of my parents' deck, wearing a yellow sweater, his thick gray hair combed neatly back. He was looking up into the sky, a soft light falling across his face. Did he know that he would soon be journeying into a much greater mystery? As I look at that photograph, I remember my father as he was. But when I close my eyes, I am with him now—and our relationship is sweeter and closer than I could have imagined.

The unfoldment of an inner relationship with my father has been the greatest surprise and gift of my grief. I was compelled to develop this relationship during my father's illness in response to my anticipatory grief. Following the cancer diagnosis, I began to feel desperate about the distance between us; time was running out. My father went on with his life as usual, refusing to talk about this life-threatening disease.

As I agonized over his cancer and the silences in our relationship, I instinctively created a sanctuary in my bedroom, placing on a shelf next to my bed pictures of my father, flowers, and special gifts he had given me. During his illness, I sat in front of this altar every day and opened to my grief. Each time I sat in the sanctuary, I closed my eyes and opened to whatever might emerge. Images of my father spontaneously began to fill the empty space of my meditations. Fortunately, I had worked with imagination and I trusted its wisdom. I did not dismiss my experiences by telling myself, "That's just my imagination." I was comforted and inspired by my father's presence within me, even though at the time I had no idea where this would lead me.

As the weeks passed, I realized that an inner relationship was developing as my father's life was slipping away; within me we were able to talk about our past hurts and disappointments and appreciations. We talked about his dying. I held him as he convulsed with pain, and he held me as I shook with tears of grief. He was open and vulnerable in a way that had been inconceivable in our outer relationship. As this inner relationship grew stronger, I felt more accepting of the limitations of the outer one. During his last weeks of life, I was able to sit with him in the hospital, my heart open and loving. No longer waiting and hoping for the right moment to talk about our relationship, I felt at peace with him. When he lapsed into a coma, I still could connect with him inwardly.

His death in 1988 severed our outer relationship. But my father lived on within me, though death had transformed our relationship. He was softer and more vulnerable with me in my dreams and inner journeys than he had been able in life. He was wiser. When I asked him for advice about issues I was struggling with, he seemed to see invisible connections between things and had a much larger perspective. He was detached from our family dynamics and with good humor could advise me on my relationship with my mother. His old hurts didn't seem to matter to him anymore. He was also freed of the interests that had consumed him in life. In the last three decades of his life, he had felt driven to succeed in the corporate world, rising at 5 A.M. to go to work and returning home late—even after the cancer had eaten into his bones. Within me after his death, he seemed at peace with himself.

Most of us see death as an ending, a final loss. We assume that any possibility for reconciliation is gone. But this is just another concept that limits us in our grieving. For many other cultures there is no impenetrable wall to divide the living from the dead. The *New York Times* 1996 front-page article entitled "For Rural Japanese, Death Doesn't Break Family Ties" gives the example of a widow in a rural Japanese village who offers her deceased husband rice every morning and holds conversations with him, hearing his responses in her head. She is convinced that her husband changed after the logging accident that killed him nine years before and that her relationship has deepened since his death. Whereas he was once harsh and dictatorial, she finds him kinder now. "Mr. Tsujimoto may be dead, but he is certainly not gone," the article states. "As is common in Japan, he remains a respected presence in the house, regularly consulted by family members on important matters."

Sukie Miller in her book *After Death* finds a similar theme in many other cultures as well: "My research has accustomed me to the idea that a larger proportion of the world's people can access other realms. For many people realms of death are as indisputably there as San Francisco is to New Yorkers, as Africa is to Brazilians. It is a case of living within the whole of reality, not just the parts one can see. Through the vital imaginings of the people of the world, all of us can gain access to realms beyond borders" (Miller, p. 46).

Death need not cut us off from those we love. Through dreams and techniques using the imagination, we can access an inner relationship with a deceased loved one, a relationship that offers powerful and mostly untapped opportunities for healing, resolution, and even guidance. It has been my great joy to provide the tools for people to discover and explore the relationship with a deceased loved one. I have witnessed deep healings and breakthroughs as well as subtle shifts—even after years of bitterness and regret.

Very few of us ever fully express our love for another. Afraid of being hurt, we find ourselves unwilling to be as vulnerable and open as that admission requires. Despite our efforts to avoid hurts and resentments, however, they inevitably build up in our relationships with family and friends. Unaired, such hurts close our hearts and create distance between ourselves and our loved ones, increasing the difficulty even more of expressing our love and appreciation. So when a loved one dies, we may find ourselves filled with regret for all that remained unspoken. The realization that all opportunities have passed for that last talk, or even just a good-bye, can be agonizing. Many of my clients have said, about a mother, grandmother, or sister, "How I wish I had told her I loved her before she died." This kind of unfinished business can prevent us from letting go and moving on with our lives. In our grief, our old resentments, regrets, and unexpressed love can gnaw at us, creating wounds that contaminate all our other relationships.

In the afternoon of the workshop, participants worked with a series of exercises to foster a present connection with the person who had died. I urged them to be open to the relationship as it is now, not to hold on to past memories which freeze the relationship into the past and make it difficult if not impossible to experience any shifts or changes that have taken place since the death. In subsequent chapters you will read some of their stories. For example, Ellen, who at first refused to focus any of the workshop exercises on a father she hated, experienced a breakthrough in her relationship with him such as she never could have imagined. And Miriam discovered answers to questions that had plagued her since her son's suicide.

Behind the group of photographs was a large window through which we could see a cherry tree aflame with red and pink blossoms, quivering with life, as though to remind us that we succumb to grief so that we can fully live. If we have grieved fully, we will emerge one day from the dark passage into a new life, seeing with new eyes, experiencing life with new vigor. Each moment becomes precious, an opportunity to embrace the wonder of life. Abraham Maslow writes, "In the postmortem life every-thing gets precious, gets piercingly important. You get stabbed by things, by flowers and by babies and by beautiful things." As I looked at those tender, translucent blossoms throughout the day, I couldn't help feeling stabbed by their beauty—transitory as it was.

As I packed up my notes at the end of the day, slipping the picture of my father into the pocket of my briefcase, I felt profoundly grateful to him for making it possible for me to do this work. It is grace to be with those who are grieving—everything is stripped bare and there is room for humanness and mystery. I am continually reminded of the power of the human spirit to heal and of the new beginnings in every ending.

Shortly after that workshop I visited with my father in my imagina-tion. It had been years since his death and months since our last visit, and I was overjoyed to see him. I often don't realize how much I miss him in my everyday life until I am once again in his presence. This time he spoke about love—how love is within us and all around us, that if it were not for love the electrons would not move in their orbits nor the stars in the heavens. He squeezed my hand—love too has guided the evolution of our relationship. We looked up. Thousands of stars shimmered above us against a black backdrop of space. Standing there beside him under a dome of limitless stars, I felt surrounded by mystery and profoundly grateful that he lives on within me.

To the imagination, death is not an ending, not a catastrophe but a transformation. Within you, your loved one lives on, and with your par-ticipation, your mutual relationship will grow and change. In this book, I will help you to reach this special relationship through your imagina-tion, using practical, effective methods to resolve old hurts, share your appreciations and disappointments, express your sometimes pure yet sometimes ambivalent love, and update your relationships by integrat-ing the changes and new insights that have occurred to you since your loved one's death.

As you work with the exercises in this book, try to set aside your assumptions and expectations. Note especially as we proceed that it is important to keep old images and memories from dictating the nature of the relationship after death. Be open to new possibilities. You have the power within yourself to create and re-create your relationships, to heal old wounds, to experience deep intimacy. Reconnect with your beloved, restore the lost dialogue, transform an absence into a presence. All that is keeping you from a sense of connection with your loved one is your unused imagination.

It is my hope that you will use the techniques in this book to restore communication and open your heart to a transformed relationship. Death is an ending, but it is also a beginning. The future is still open. Your lost beloved is within reach—within *you*—much closer than you think. It is my hope that when your loved one stands at the threshold, offering you the gift of an inner relationship, you will open the door of the imagination.

Part One
Looking Within

The presence of that absence is everywhere.

Edna St. Vincent Millay

1

The Living Presence within You

*I began to feel that all the people I'd ever known who had died
or left me had not in fact gone away, but continued to live on inside me
just as this man's wife lived on inside him.*
Arthur Golden

When a loved one dies, many people are filled with regret for all that was never expressed between them. It can be agonizing to realize that all opportunities are gone for that last talk, the chance to say the unsaid and tie up loose ends. With old hurts unhealed, good-byes unspoken, or love unexpressed, the result can be frustration, guilt, bitterness, obsessive thinking—even an inability to get on with one's life.

In their regret, people often go over and over their last encounter with a loved one, focusing with excruciating detail on what was and was not said. Again and again clients tell me,

- "How I wish I had told him I loved him before he died."
- "I wish I hadn't said so many hurtful things that day. I didn't know it would be our last talk."
- "I was in such a hurry. It was one of the few days when I stayed only for a little while, and we hardly spoke at all."

So many regrets: that one hadn't been present at the moment of death; that there had been no chance to say good-bye; that so many chances for meaningful interaction had been overlooked; that there had been so many times long before the dying when one had forgotten to call or write or had put off doing so. But in my experience, the deepest regret—and the one with the sharpest sting—attends the failure to say, "I love you." This seems to be the most important message we can communicate to each other—and too often we feel there's so much time to express our love that we simply put off doing so.

Marta came to one of my "Losing a Parent" workshops, and she shared with the group that in grieving the death of her father she was consumed with regret and self-blame. Dismayed by her father's alcoholism and abusive conduct, she had cut off contact with him months before he died. She felt that by distancing herself from her father she would develop healthier ways of relating to him once she resumed contact. Then late one night, after several months of silence, her father phoned her, sounding desperate. He was drunk, his words slurred. Wanting no part of the conversation, she told him she would talk to him when he was sober and hung up the phone. The next morning the police called Marta to inform her that her father had been found dead in his apartment. She was devastated.

Months later, she still felt so overwhelmed by regret and guilt that she was having difficulty functioning in her daily life. "If only I had gone to his house that night," she told us, "he might still be alive today. I feel so terrible and ashamed that the months I pulled away from him were the last months of his life."

Marta's situation is dramatic, but others, less clear-cut, can still be intensely painful. To assess the quality of your feelings surrounding the closure of a loved one's death, ask yourself,

- Did I express my love? Did I share my appreciations?
- Were we able to be open and honest with one another?
- What were the issues in our relationship that we did *not* talk about?
- Were there conflicts between us that remained unresolved at the death?

- Do I feel any regrets?
- Do I still harbor resentments from the past?
- Was anything left unsaid?
- Did I say good-bye?

Perhaps you are hoping that your grief will take care of itself and that your regrets will dissolve in time. Perhaps you feel that it's too late: "She's dead. What's the use?" Such hopes, as clinical practice and research show, are usually disappointed. Unresolved grief—regrets and disappointments that remain unacknowledged and unaddressed—continues to work silently and insidiously within the person left behind, resulting in such symptoms as apathy, social isolation, addiction, chronic physical problems, fearfulness, depression, overworking, and compulsive behavior. The antidote to these symptoms is to look, open-eyed, at the leave-taking once more in order to identify and resolve unaddressed issues.

In this chapter, I introduce two concepts that can change your perception of loss forever:

1. Your loved one lives on within you.
2. And you can gain access to this relationship through your imagination.

I also introduce a powerful method based on these principles that will enable you to communicate *internally* with your deceased loved one and resolve unfinished business, express your love, and feel more at peace with yourself. In later chapters we'll be concerned with technique—how, in practical terms, to put these principles to work. For now, however, in this introductory chapter, my goal is to reassure you that the tools do indeed exist for reconnecting with the person you may have considered lost forever.

Just Behind the Door

Most of us see death as an ending, a final loss. We assume that a door has closed, that our loved one has gone, and that gone, too, are any possibilities for reconciliation. It *is* true that the old relationship has come to an end. You will never again be in the physical presence of the person. However, death need not cut you off from those you love. An *inner* relationship with the person who has died continues on after death. This relationship, constantly unfolding within, offers powerful and mostly untapped opportunities for healing, resolution, and even guidance. It is said that every ending brings a new beginning. So it is that the end of a life can bring a new beginning in your relationship with the person you consider lost to you forever.

For many, this concept is new and hard to accept. You may resist the idea at first, but if you're willing to experiment with the methods presented in this book, you will experience this inner relationship directly. Once that happens, you will never again doubt that your beloved lives on—within you.

You may have already had a dream or dreams about the person, dreams that seemed so real that you have awakened wondering whether he or she were still alive after all. Dreams often give us the first glimpses of this ongoing relationship. Psychologist Carl Jung had this reaction when he dreamed about his deceased father six weeks after the elder's death:

> Suddenly he stood before me and said that he was coming back from his holiday. He had made a good recovery and was now coming home. I thought he would be annoyed with me for having moved into his room. But not a bit of it! Nevertheless, I felt ashamed because I had imagined he was dead.... Later I kept asking myself: 'What does it mean that my father returns in dreams and that he seems so real?' It was an unforgettable experience, and it forced me for the first time to think about life after death (Jung, p. 96).

In an example closer to home, the night after his death, the husband of Brenda, a workshop participant, appeared to her in a dream. When Brenda expressed surprise that her husband stood before her, radiant and healthy, he gently admonished her, "I never left you." Many such dreams share a common theme: The deceased takes for granted that the relationship is ongoing, while the griever/dreamer struggles to accept this new concept.

How common are these dreams? Numerous studies have focused on after-death contacts. In 1984, the National Opinion Research Council conducted a general public survey of contact experiences with the dead. Sixty-seven percent of people with deceased spouses reported such contacts, while 42 percent of the general public makes such claims. In 1976, researchers Kalish and Reynolds wrote about after-death contacts in their book *Death and Ethnicity*. According to this research, 50 percent of women and 30 percent of men reported after-death contacts, and the most commonly reported form was through dreams.

I myself cannot be sure if these experiences involve actual contact with the dead—no one can. But the very existence of these contact experiences attests to the fact that our loved ones live on in us in the form of an inner presence. Rather than debate about the "reality" of these experiences, let us focus on those indisputable inner relationships with our deceased loved ones, developing them, deepening them, and learning to enjoy them. The door into these places of contact is the imagination, as the story of Gail, a participant in one of my dream groups, dramatically illustrates.

Gail's Story

Gail was devastated when her cousin Peter was killed in a 1994 American Eagle crash. Although she has experienced eight other deaths since that time, Peter's death was the hardest for her to grieve. She had loved her cousin deeply and had no opportunity to prepare for his death or say good-bye to him. When she thought of him, she pictured mangled body parts scattered over a field in Indiana.

Shortly after his death, Gail had a dream in which Peter was standing inside a glass dome. Separated from her by this invisible barrier, Gail could hear him tell her that he was OK, but she agonized that she could not reach him. After three years, Gail felt ready to face her grief and explored with me several significant dreams involving Peter, one of which was a breakthrough.

In this dream, Peter was present at a family Thanksgiving gathering. Gail was comforted by Peter's presence in the room, although he did not engage in conversations but stood silently at the periphery. When it came time to part, Gail approached Peter and shared with him how devastating his death had been for her. Holding one another, they cried together and expressed how much they missed each other. However, it was Peter's touch that had the most profound impact on Gail. Before that hug, everything about death had seemed so far away, and Peter had seemed unreachable and untouchable. That moment of touch restored Peter to her as a living inner presence. And ironically, contacting Peter in this way enabled her to finally say good-bye to him and release him as he had been.

The next morning she could still feel the warmth of that hug, and she lay awake savoring it. She knew that the struggle had lifted; nothing was now left unfinished. That dream had been an epiphany, transforming not only her relationship to Peter but also her relationship to her grief. It would continue to surface from time to time, but her grief no longer frightened her. For the first time, she felt that she could visit the field where the crash had taken place.

Imagination: the Bridge

In making contact as Gail did with her cousin Peter, imagination is the bridge, connecting our external reality and the internal world of our psyche. With our loved ones present within us, imagination renders death not an ending but a transformation.

Irish poet and author John O'Donohue tells us that imagination is the most neglected spiritual faculty in the Western intellect. We can't talk about death and grief, he insists, without talking about the imagination; indeed, the riches of these huge adjacencies won't be available to us until we claim the imagination.

Many other cultures have turned to the imagination as a valuable resource for grieving. In *Imagery in Healing*, author Dr. Jeanne Achterberg calls the imagination our "oldest and greatest healing resource" (Achterberg, p. 3). For thousands of years, shamans throughout the world have traveled in a trance state into invisible worlds to consult with the spirits of the deceased and have served as messengers between the worlds. The *Tibetan Book of the Dead* provides texts for the living to read to the deceased that describe what to expect, what to avoid, and what to look for in the transitional states after death. The Confucian and Buddhist religions teach that each household should have an altar that is dedicated to the family ancestors. Daily observance at this altar facilitates ongoing contact with the deceased. The living family members converse with the photographs set on the altar and place gifts there for the dead. In exchange, the ancestors are expected to maintain a living presence in the house, providing guidance and inspiration.

In the Middle Ages, the common practice of holding conversations with the souls of the departed provided comfort and reassurance to those who were grieving. The Swiss-German physician and alchemist Paraclesus wrote, "Everyone can educate and regulate his imagination so as to come thereby into contact with spirits, and be taught by them."

In contemporary Australia, Aborigines continue the ancient practice of talking to the spirit emerging from rocks that have been rubbed together for three days. The Aborigines believe that their dead ancestors return to share both mythic and practical information. In many cultures, then, death is no barrier to communication, because people actively utilize the imagination when faced with this inevitable transition.

Many myths remind us that our relationship with a beloved can be restored, even when death has occurred. Think of the Egyptian goddess Isis and her husband/brother Osiris. Osiris, having been killed by conspirators, is locked in a coffin and sent down the Nile. In a state of deep grief, Isis searches and finally finds her husband's body. However, while she is visiting with her son, one of the conspirators cuts up the body and scatters the pieces. With the help of the gods, Isis pieces the body together and Osiris comes back to life. He then reigns as king of the dead in the Underworld.

The Greek myth of Demeter and Persephone presents a similar theme. When Persephone is abducted into the Underworld by the god of death, her mother Demeter is devastated with grief and refuses to allow any vegetation to grow on earth. She bargains with the gods of Olympus for her daughter's return, and with the help of the messenger god, Persephone and Demeter are reunited. However, since Persephone has eaten three pomegranate seeds before leaving Hades, she must spend three months a year in the Underworld, where she reigns as queen.

Most ancient cultures have myths conveying the interwoven themes of loss, search, and recovery, as if to remind people that it is possible to reconnect with deceased loved ones. But in our modern world, which values technology over tribal practices, the power and even the existence of invisible worlds has been denied. Imagination has been relegated to fantasy and at times considered abnormal. "Oh, it's just your imagination," people tell us condescendingly. And so our most valuable resource in the grieving process has been devalued and all but lost to us.

The methods described in this book are designed to help nurture your power of imagination. You may argue that you just aren't an imaginative person, but be assured that imagination is a natural and universal faculty. Everyone has it, though in many it remains muted and undeveloped.

Many authors and practitioners in many different fields, including modern medicine and psychology, have researched, written about, and used imagination in their work with clients. All have come to a similar conclusion: Imagination has been an important resource for healing since the beginning of history, and it is time for our culture to acknowledge its usefulness for healing both body and psyche. All the techniques you'll learn in subsequent chapters are tied to the use of imagination in nurturing and deepening your inner communication.

Fostering Your Imagination

Though imagination is part of our psychic birthright, many people have let this powerful faculty go dormant. However, certain psychological states such as grief and depression seem to activate the imagination naturally. People who are grieving find that they have little energy or enthusiasm for external reality; their energy is drawn inward. And as grief dampens their outer senses, it can open *inner* senses, giving them new acuity in seeing, hearing, and feeling what is inaccessible to our senses during normal times.

After her husband's death, the world looked dull and flat to Brenda. However, when she slept, her dreams burst with vivid imagery and vibrant colors. In a workshop setting, she followed my instructions to take her time to fully experience the sights, sounds, and smells of an imaginary house, and she readily made the transition to an inner world where she had a profoundly moving encounter with her husband. Experiencing this inner world directly through her senses definitely fostered her imagination.

Psychologist Jean Houston affirms that wounding can open the doors of our sensibility to a larger reality, one that we usually fail to perceive. In my grief workshops, I have been struck with the ease and openness with which participants are able to work with exercises involving the imagination—even participants who have long considered themselves not to be highly imaginative. People who rarely remember their dreams may report vivid dreams when they are grieving.

However, although grief may jump-start the inner senses, most people who do not regularly use the imagination find that it takes concentration and energy to awaken atrophied senses fully. If you have ever had to work on atrophied muscles after weeks of disuse, you know what effort is required. The same is true when you begin to work on activating the inner senses: You may get discouraged because you can't "see" anything. In this context, it is unfortunate that such activation is often associated with the visualization of imagery. The fact is that not everyone visualizes; in fact, about 40 percent do not. Many people *do* experience imagery through hearing, touch, or movement, but others just "sense things." Even if you *can* visualize, "Seeing into the other world requires a different kind of seeing that we have almost, it seems, forgotten how to do" (Larsen, p. xix). While one sense may naturally be stronger, I encourage you to work on activating *all* your inner senses. The following exercise will help you do this. Remember that this important step of awakening your inner senses will facilitate the flow and vividness of your imagination.

Exercise 1-1
AWAKENING YOUR INNER SENSES

Close your eyes. Let your attention first focus on your breathing. Be aware of the sensations you experience with every inhalation and exhalation. Now imagine yourself standing in the center of a kitchen. There is an open fireplace in one corner. You can hear the crackling of the fire. Move closer and hold up your hands to the fire. Feel the heat. Look closely at the colors in the flames. A pot is simmering on an iron stand in the fireplace, and soup is bubbling over. Smell the aromas. Focus on this, seeing if you can identify what is cooking. You might even be able to smell the herbs flavoring the soup. There is a wooden spoon sitting next to the pot. Pick it up, feeling its texture and weight. Dip it into the pot of soup and scoop out some to taste. Savor it in your mouth, feeling your taste buds responding.

In the imagination, we are not limited to the laws of ordinary reality. There we can fly, we can change form, we can do things that would be impossible in daily life. It takes a while to adjust and open fully to these freedoms, freedoms that enable us to experience relationships from new perspectives. Be willing to let go of your expectations regarding the limitations of daily life. Consider the benefits of crossing the border of "the possible" in this story of a client:

Susan had been frightened of her domineering father ever since she was a little girl. Even as an adult she avoided talking to him about anything that might provoke his wrath. After her father's death, she felt angry at herself for her lack of courage and for her passivity in her relationship with him. She never felt free of him—only haunted by all that had been left unsaid. In a therapy session, she decided to work with her imagination in order finally to confront her father. Closing her eyes, she saw him in his red plaid shirt standing before her. Being a tall man, he towered over her, and she felt as small and vulnerable as she had as a child. A familiar feeling of paralysis overtook her, and she was unable to speak. Suddenly she discovered that she was slowly rising up off the floor, until she was looking eye-to-eye with her father. From this new perspective, Susan felt safer, stronger, and clearer. She voiced all the feelings, resentments, and longings she had held back from him. As she talked, she noticed something stirring in her chest that she had never felt in her father's presence before—tenderness. If she had interrupted the flow of imagination by saying, "But I can't do this! I can't fly!" she would not have had this experience of healing.

It is important to approach the imagination with a nonjudgmental, nonanalytical, receptive awareness. So many times my clients will judge or edit what is happening as they explore the imagination. They try to change an image because they don't understand or don't like it. This interference inhibits the richness, wisdom, and mystery of the imagination.

Last but not least, approach the imagination with respect. This faculty is enormously powerful. In 1942, during World War II, Carl Jung gave a lecture on "Der Geist Mercurius" (the Spirit Mercury), in which he warned that imagination could be a force either of healing or of destruction. To illustrate, he told a story from the brothers Grimm called "The Spirit in the Bottle," which I paraphrase here:

A young man was so poor that he was unable to complete his education. One day he found a bottle, from which a voice cried out, "Let me out!" The man opened the bottle and a mighty spirit rose up, as big as the oak tree under which the bottle had lain. The spirit spoke to him, "I am the powerful Mercury," boomed the spirit. "I was shut up in this bottle as penance. Whoever lets me loose, I will break his neck." The young man realized that his only hope in saving his life was to entice the spirit back into the bottle. "I cannot believe that such a mighty spirit could come out of such a little bottle," he told the spirit with awe. "Could you show me how you did that?" The spirit immediately obliged, and the young man rammed the stopper back into the bottle. With that the situation had changed: Mercury was contained, but this time the young man was aware of his power. The spirit begged the young man to free him again, but now in exchange for a reward, a cloth that would turn anything it rubbed into silver. Pleased with this exchange, the young man set the spirit free. Using the cloth to create silver, he made enough money to complete his studies and became a famous doctor.

This story demonstrates the need to approach Mercury, the spirit of imagination, with great respect. Otherwise, he can become destructive. At first the young man does not know of Mercury's great powers, so when he releases the spirit he endangers himself. To save himself from destruction, he must find a way to contain the power. Only then can he begin to work with Mercury to his benefit. And to do that, he must communicate with Mercury and work out a mutually satisfactory relationship. That done, he can dare to let the power out of the bottle again, this time in the service of healing, using Mercury's powers to become a doctor. The young man is now richer than he was—and wiser. In order to use the gift of imagination to help you heal your relationships, you must be humble in its presence and respectful of its power.

Common Problems

Some people have difficulty working with the imagination, especially in the beginning. If this is true for you, it will help you to know that you will go through three different stages as you develop your capacity to work with the imagination. In the first stage, many people struggle, unable to imagine, see, hear, touch, or sense anything out of the ordinary. In this stage, simply remind yourself that imagination is a natural faculty, that *everyone* has it, and that it is accessible within you. If you work toward activating your inner senses persistently and patiently, they will gradually strengthen. You may not be able to *see* actual images that are inaccessible in the ordinary world, but you may be able to sense or even hear things. Pay careful attention to everything that happens, no matter how subtle or insignificant.

In the second stage, you *will* begin to experience imagery, but you may question it and ask yourself, Am I making this up? Is this real? Realize that this questioning, which often interrupts the flow of imagery, is a completely normal response. Notice that you are doubting your experience, but don't let your doubts stop you from exploring. Remember: This is just a stage, one that most people pass through as their imagination continues to develop.

In the third stage, images will begin to occur spontaneously and uninhibitedly. Now you may realize that the world you are exploring in the imagination is as real as anything you have experienced in ordinary reality. Jungian analyst Mary Watkins expressed this succinctly: "Going into the imaginal then becomes not a matter of preserving oneself in a foreign land but rather of returning home" (Watkins, p. 118).

Be patient and thorough as you develop imagination skills. You are preparing to meet and interact with a deceased loved one. Imagination will enable you to walk across the silent chasm of death—and touch, see, and talk with this person.

The Need for Dialogue

Psychologist Louise Kaplan asserts in her book *No Voice Is Ever Wholly Lost* that "dialogue is the heartbeat of human existence . . . we cannot live without it" (Kaplan, p. 239). She sees this factor as playing such a pivotal role in our lives that we dread the loss of it more than actual extinction.

Much has been written in the field of developmental psychology that confirms the critical importance of dialogue even in the earliest days of infancy. In this context, it's easy to understand how the cessation of dialogue when a loved one dies can be devastating. "We cripple our own selves and even destroy the world around us in our desperate quest to refind, recover, restore, reconstitute a lost dialogue" (Kaplan, p. 239). When our efforts to reconnect fail, we may feel helpless to resolve unfinished business and unable to reach peace with our loss.

Many people secretly or unconsciously attempt to carry on a lost dialogue with a loved one. For example, a person might talk to a deceased spouse over morning coffee. A grieving mother may converse with her deceased child while sorting through his toys or clothes. Often people keep these communications secret for fear of being misunderstood by the living. Or they hold these conversations without any understanding of the rich possibilities for healing.

Shortly after the publication of my book *Your Loved One Lives On within You*, a woman introduced herself to me at the Capitola Book Cafe. Lira's thirty-year-old son had died of a heart attack six months before. Since her son's death, she had talked with him daily—and often heard his responses in her head. Although these dialogues felt natural and healing to her, she was upset that her husband dismissed her experiences, even to the point of rolling his eyes when she spoke about them. She had learned to keep her experiences to herself, but now Lira worried that they were abnormal. She felt ashamed and confused. As I helped her understand her dialogues with her son in a new context—that her son lives on within her and that she instinctively has been nurturing her inner relationship with him through her dialogues—she brightened with relief. I encouraged her to continue exploring this relationship with her son and suggested some exercises. As we parted, she gave me a warm hug and told me, "I can't tell you what this has meant to me. I trust my own experience now." Many of us stumble across this inner relationship but don't trust it or know how to consciously work with it to maximize healing.

If dialogue is so critical for our well-being and existence, how can we recover a dialogue that has been lost through the death of a loved one? How can we transform an absence into a presence? The answer is by vitalizing our urge to communicate with our developing imagination. In this way, we gain access directly to the beloved.

Internal Communication

How, specifically, can we make that dreamed-of contact? Simply exhorting you to "use your imagination!" is too vague, but an effective, easy-to-learn method exists to enable you to reach the presence within. Internal communication is a powerful tool that utilizes the imagination to resolve old hurts and resentments, express love, adjust the relationship to its new context and circumstances, and feel more at peace with deceased loved ones. Such communication takes place inside you, opening up significant possibilities for the relationship that actually go far beyond the scope of the sort of everyday, external communication you are used to.

Communication is the single greatest factor affecting our relationships with family members. Not only for practical reasons and to keep the family running smoothly but for our health and well-being, it is critical that we express our love, work through our anger and differences, and resolve particularly disturbing issues with those we cherish. For many people, however, the greater the difficulties within their relationships, the harder it is to talk freely. In most families, certain important issues and past events just aren't discussed, and members consider it unsafe to express, disagree about, or even confront the truth. Family therapist Virginia Satir writes in *The New Peoplemaking* that only 4.5 percent of the population are emotionally honest in their communications with family members; the rest cover up their true feelings, creating distance and mistrust in their relationships, undermining their self-worth, and building anxiety and stress.

But as you will experience soon, encounters using internal communication techniques differ greatly from encounters in everyday life. Even if you are among those who resist full *external* communication, you will find that freely expressing yourself internally is not only possible but enjoyable. Here, inside, you can address unresolved aspects of a relationship—not merely a relationship with a deceased person but with *anyone*—voice repressed feelings, deepen bonds, heal rifts, and feel more compassion for the other person—all in privacy without the other person's external presence. You'll learn to "step inside" the other person to gain valuable insights into the other's feelings and point of view. When you practice internal communication with the person you have lost, you'll experience both the release of what has been bottled up inside and more peace with the loss as the love you feel begins to flow freely to its object.

As with any communication technique, the quality of internal communication depends on certain commitments from you:

- The resolve to proceed
- The promise to *listen* carefully as well as to speak out

· The willingness to take responsibility for your own feelings and avoid blaming, insulting, manipulating, and demanding

If you have hurts or resentments you want to communicate, be prepared to slow down and describe them so that your loved one can understand. If you feel angry, it will be most effective if you are specific. When it is your turn to listen, try to be as receptive, relaxed, and empathetic as you can. Ask thoughtful questions so that you can better understand the other's point of view. Acknowledge the feelings underlying the words as well as the content. This interaction is not a power struggle—the point is not to prove right or wrong but to reopen, exchange, listen, weigh, and see old issues with fresh eyes.

In communication with the deceased, changing old patterns of interacting may not be as hard as it sounds. You may be surprised to discover that the person, and the relationship too, as experienced in the imagination, have changed greatly. For example,

· In the physical body, the person may appear younger, healthier, and more vital than when alive.
· In the personality, the person may act with less ego, more compassion, and more objectivity and may be less likely to get caught up in family dynamics.
· In values and perspectives, old interests, even ones that were consuming passions in life, may evaporate, and more concern for spiritual matters may be in evidence.

One of my clients, Doreen, found in a dream shortly after her father's death that he had changed dramatically. Robert looked healthy and vital, though when he died his body had been ravaged by cancer. In the dream he was surrounded by the family, each member desperately asking financial questions about the estate. This made sense, since Robert had been very involved in investing and controlling the family finances, and the family still looked to him for advice and guidance. However, now he seemed completely disinterested. Waving all the questions aside, he said, "These things don't concern me now."

In chapters 4, 5, and 6, I suggest how such changes can help create breakthroughs in communication that seemed impossible before. For now, simply ready yourself to be open and receptive to changes in your loved one and to let yourself relinquish old pictures of the relationship.

It is important, too, that you approach internal communication free of preconceived ideas of the content and outcome of each encounter, since expectations can limit the vast range of the imagination. More often than not, the interactions with deceased loved ones will differ markedly from what you anticipate. Most people are pleasantly surprised both by what they discover in their inner encounters—and, later, by outer events in their daily lives.

Consider Joseph, who was devastated by his brother Jim's death. The two had had a stormy relationship, and Jim's death appeared to end any possibility for reconciliation. When I suggested in a therapy session that Joseph use internal communication to gain access to his ongoing relationship with Jim, he was very skeptical. He assumed that he would be incapable of using his imagination effectively and that, even if he *could* reach Jim through his imagination, his brother would be as antagonistic as he had always been in life. Reluctantly, though, Joseph tried exercise 6-2, "The Rose," in chapter 6. He was surprised not only by how vividly he saw Jim in his imagination but also by the warmth and love with which his brother greeted him. The two spoke at length about their relationship, a conversation that Joseph had longed for all his adult life, and Jim shared some childhood resentments that had poisoned his feelings for Joseph—resentments that stemmed from their parents' clear favoring of Joseph. After completing this exercise, Joseph not only felt loving and forgiving toward Jim but sensed a new comfort in himself that felt significant and permanent.

Timeless Rewards

The great Chilean-American novelist Isabel Allende told her publisher that she felt her writing career would end when her mother died, since her mother had always edited all her books. Her publisher reminded her that her mother was already inside her. Wrote Allende, "I realized he's right. Absolutely right. I will always be able to say, Okay, here I have a terrible sentence and my mother will come back to me. . . . I hope that when I die I will have been able to, during my life, plant little seeds in the souls of my children and my grandchildren so that when they need something from me I will always be available" (Epel, p. 23). How comforting to have this understanding before a loved one's death! I have seen many others make similar breakthroughs and reach life-changing insights by reaching the beloved within, healing old wounds, bringing the relationship up to date, and finally saying good-bye.

Succeeding chapters guide you in putting internal communication into practice. We begin simply, with exercises designed to help you express whatever has been concealed, held back, or repressed. Gradually, you will learn to have inner dialogues with the person you are missing. And in part three, you'll learn to use internal communication techniques to ease communication problems with grieving family members.

It is never too late to reconcile with a loved one, whether living or dead. As I will discuss in more detail in chapter 5, one eighty-two-year-old woman used the techniques described in this book to heal old wounds in her relationship with her father. He had died more than forty years before. The thread of that relationship had seemed to disappear for all those years, but it was hidden in the fabric of her life. The reemergence of that thread through spontaneous dialogue transformed an absence into a presence and inspired her to creativity she hadn't known before. To gather up that thread and follow it to its source is to link our finite lives with the infinite, to nourish our souls with mystery.

The ways of imagining and communicating introduced here are gifts you will carry forever. Only open to them, reflect on them with patience and trust, and allow the possibility that they will work for you as you hope they will. The results could ease your pain and enrich your life forever.

Part Two

Reaching Within

And what the dead had no speech for, when living,
They can tell you being dead:
The communication of the dead is tongued with fire
beyond the language of the living.

T. S. Eliot

2

Communicating with One Who Is Dying

There is a land of the living and a land of the dead and the bridge is love,
the only survival, the only meaning.
Thornton Wilder

Deena quietly entered the stark hospital room and took a seat next to her mother's bed. Although it had been just a few days since her last visit, Deena was shocked at how emaciated her mother looked, her pale skin drawn tightly over the protruding bones of her face. She was sleeping, her labored breathing suggesting that pain was disturbing her rest. It was still hard for Deena to comprehend that this frail and helpless person was her mother. When Deena was a child, the outspoken and energetic Angela had seemed larger than life. Deena had adored Angela for these qualities—though as a teenager she had abhorred them. From the time she turned twelve, Deena was embarrassed to be seen with her mother in public, feeling hypercritical of the way her mother dressed, talked, and walked—everything! It was then that Deena stopped talking to her mother about anything that really mattered to her. Mother and daughter fought viciously during those years. Eventually, they learned to relate cordially though distantly, but the original closeness never returned.

Now Angela was dying of breast cancer. Deena longed to talk to her, sharing her disappointments and joys and expressing her love. As Deena thought about this seeming impossibility, Angela stirred beneath the white sheets and opened her eyes. For a few precious minutes she looked tenderly into her daughter's face. Deena reached for her mother's hand, pressing the cool bony flesh into her own. "I'm here, Mom. I've missed you. I . . ." Her voice trailed off as she perceived that Angela suddenly seemed to be staring through her—as though some invisible presence had once again drawn away her mother's attention. Frustrated, Deena felt her chest tighten. She had really hoped to *talk* to her mother on this visit. There was so much she wanted to share with her—regrets, appreciations, recent realizations about their relationship, love.

Still staring into the distance, her mother softly mumbled, "I'm going on a trip soon. I need to get ready." This statement confused Deena. What was her mother talking about? She had made such statements before. Why did she keep telling her that she was going on a trip? She was too sick to even think about traveling! Last week when Angela had made a similar statement, Deena had tried to reason with her. "You're in the hospital, Mom. You need to save your energy for trying to get better." Angela had become very agitated, pulling at the sheets and trying to get out of bed. This time, so as not to upset her mother again, Deena remained silent.

Sitting with a family member who is in the final stages of dying can be excruciating—especially when one thinks about all that has never been said. Both the caring family members and the dying person may feel the urgent need to reconcile and yet still be unable to communicate in anything but short, unsatisfactory fragments. Too little energy, too little time— the sheer physical limits often defeat the most intense desire. Deena knew that her time to talk with her mother was quickly running out; even when Angela was awake and aware, she could focus only for brief periods. Still, both knew instinctively that using what little time and energy were left to express love to each other could produce some of life's most meaningful moments. Simply the mutual urge to try was a healing bond between them.

How the Dying Communicate

It can come as a surprise to the living, but communication is a critical part of the dying process. And yet communication with people on their deathbeds can be frustrating, confusing, and disorienting. Dying people seem absorbed in another realm, drifting in and out of contact with the living. When they look at us, their eyes are often glassy, unfocused; sometimes they seem to look right through us. People close to death may converse with invisible beings—perhaps dead friends or relatives—and speak of invisible places. Henri Nouwen, reflecting on his time with his dying mother, wrote in *In Memoriam*, "She was seeing other realities, more awesome, more frightening, more captivating, but also more decisive" (Nouwen, p. 22).

Those who are dying may talk in symbols, and they may act frustrated and restless when we cannot understand them. In the days before my father went into a coma, he tried constantly to get out of the hospital bed "to go home." I thought at that time that "home" meant my parents' house, some thirty minutes from the hospital. Now I realize that he meant something much more subtle—the return to a source.

Maggie Callanan and Patricia Kelley are hospice nurses who have written an important book on communicating with the dying called *Final Gifts*. They challenge the common assumptions that the dying are "out of it" or "confused," maintaining that these responses only serve to create more distance between the dying and their family and friends. These two pioneers carefully researched their patients' communications and realized that the dying often use symbolic language to describe what they are experiencing and to express their desire for a peaceful death. Callanan and Kelley insist that if we pay close attention to everything the dying person says and does, we may begin to understand the messages. Cicely Saunders, a founder of the hospice movement in England, wrote, "I once asked a man who knew he was dying what he needed above all from those caring for him. He said 'For someone to look at me as if they were trying to understand me'" (Saunders, p. 3).

To help make these last, precious opportunities for interaction rich with meaning and understanding, I offer the following suggestions for communicating with a dying loved one:

- Pay close attention to whatever a dying person says or does, since he or she may be trying to communicate an important message to you.
- Validate what the person is saying to you, even if you don't completely understand the message. Learn to listen without judging. Look for signs of frustration or agitation that may indicate you are misinterpreting the message.
- Let your loved one know when you are confused. Ask questions that reflect a genuine desire to understand what the dying person is experiencing. Give reassurance that you understand how difficult it is for the person to communicate with you.
- Watch for nonverbal cues. These may be subtle. The dying person may squeeze your hand, raise an eyebrow, tighten muscles, breathe faster or slower, or make a sound.
- If you feel at a loss for words, or if words seem to get in the way of a deeper connection, simply sit with the person in silence. Much can be communicated through a reassuring and loving touch. You can also speak silently "through your heart."

Just as the dying person may feel an urgency to communicate to you, so you may feel an urgency to communicate back in order to reconcile your relationship, express love, and resolve old hurts. Don't let the chance pass you by. Transcend any natural reticence or embarrassment you may feel to speak clearly, heartfully, and concisely. But be careful not to impose subjects on the person that you sense are too painful or uncomfortable. You can explore these matters later, on your own, using internal communication.

Because time is short and the actual exchanges you manage may be frustrating or unsatisfying, it can be helpful to work with internal communication even at the deathbed. As I sat next to my father in the hospital, I wanted to talk about his dying since this had stirred up so many feelings about our relationship. But from the moment he heard that he had cancer, he had refused to talk about dying. At first this caused me anguish, but I learned to talk with him about these topics in my imagination, resolving many of the resentments and hurts that had kept my heart so closed and protected in our adult relationship. Through this practice, I was able to be fully present, relaxed, and loving with my father in his last days. Before I attained these new possibilities for communication, I felt tense and expectant whenever I was with him, waiting and hoping for the right moment to talk about our relationship. But after talking with him in my imagination, I felt at peace just sitting with him in silence. My work with imagination during this time had given me a priceless gift.

The series of exercises and suggestions that follow will help you explore ways of communicating internally with a dying person. Feel free to do all the exercises in the order they are presented, or just try the ones that you feel most drawn to. To get the best results, set aside an uninterrupted time in a special place. Think of this retreat place—a room in your own home—as a sanctuary. Choose a place where you feel safe and secure and where you can be alone. Set up an altar there with pictures, special objects, or drawings of the person who is dying.

So that you won't be interrupted, put a note on the door and take your phone off the hook. Then sit down before your altar, close your eyes, and focus on your breathing for a few minutes to settle your body and mind. Reserve thirty minutes to an hour for performing each exercise, doing only one per session. When you have completed each exercise, write down what happened to provide a record of events, help you integrate any insights, and give you the opportunity later to observe and interpret the changes occurring within yourself.

The sanctuary, though simple in concept, is a very potent place of healing. For years my clients have retreated to their sanctuaries as a profoundly significant part of their process of coping with the dying and death of people close to them. Even after only a week of using the sanctuary, clients consistently report feeling more at peace, less overwhelmed by their emotions, and more able to attend to other obligations in their lives.

If you visit your sanctuary at least once a week (with more visits as you feel the need), it will be much easier to shift gears from the external world and focus on internal communication. Visiting it every week will build concentration while maintaining a sense of continuity.

Exercise 2-1
INTERNAL COMMUNICATION WITH THE DYING

Relaxed in your sanctuary, close your eyes, and in your mind's eye visualize entering the room in which the person is dying. Sit down next to the bed. Take a few minutes to experience this room with all your senses. What do you see around you? What can you hear? Are there any smells? Take the person's hand and feel its weight, its temperature, and its texture. With a squeeze of the hand or with your words, let him or her know that you have come to visit. You now have the opportunity to communicate with this person in a way that you never really considered possible before. You can express everything that you want to in order to help resolve conflicts in your relationship.

Picture yourself expressing your love and appreciation as well as your disappointments, regrets, and hurts. Next, in your imagination, listen carefully and respectfully to what your loved one has to say to you. Continue your dialogue until it feels complete. You may then want to spend some time together in silence. When you feel ready to leave, say good-bye and leave the room. Open your eyes and savor your feelings for a few minutes. Then record your experience in the journal reserved for this purpose.

Deena's Experience
Deena consulted with me during the period in which Angela was dying. She realized how important it was to share with Angela the love, appreci-

ations, and disappointments she had held back for so many years. For more than thirty years, mother and daughter had avoided talking about their relationship. Too many times they had been silent about the little hurts and misunderstandings that had built up, as such impediments inevitably do, between two people. Ironically, just as Deena was beginning to feel ready to communicate with her mother, Angela began losing the ability to maintain contact for any length of time. Discussing her predicament with me, Deena expressed her frustration. She had hoped for the relief of finally having her say.

When I introduced the concept of internal communication, Deena saw immediately that channels of communication were open to her that she had not considered before. She agreed to try exercise 2-1, above, and saw that it offered an opportunity to work through her own unresolved issues so that she could sit with Angela peacefully and lovingly as she died. Here's the account Deena wrote in her exercise journal of her experience in performing exercise 2-1:

> I entered the room. The late afternoon light was streaming across the bed, illuminating the form of Mother's frail body under the white blanket. She was wide awake, which surprised me. Her gray-green eyes were fixed lovingly on me. I sat down next to her, stroked her hand, and told her, "Mother, I want to take this time to really talk with you. I regret we haven't for so many years. How hard it's been for me now that I'm so ready to talk to you and you just haven't been able to. I've come into your room many times lately full of resolve to tell you what weighs on my heart. And after just a few moments you will drift off. It's so hard for me to see you dying. Mother, what am I going to do without you?" I began to cry and my mother squeezed my hand and nodded. I knew that she understood my feelings.

I felt encouraged to go on. "When I was a little girl I dreamed of growing up like you. I adored you. It seemed that you could do no wrong. Mother, we stopped talking when I was a teenager. That was such a difficult time for us. I criticized you constantly. I didn't listen to you. I talked back. I fought relentlessly with you. I needed to push you away at that time so that I could grow up. We were so close and I identified so much with you. I had to find who I was separate from you. I want you to know that I never stopped loving you, even though I stopped expressing it. I still appreciate those qualities that I adored in you when I was a little girl. I wouldn't be who I am without all the wonderful qualities you instilled in me."

My mother was crying now, tears flooding her pale cheeks. We were both speechless as we looked into each other's eyes. I felt vulnerable and raw. I let my love show. For moments I felt transported into a sacred time and space, where love flowed freely and fully. After a long while, my mother spoke quietly: "I love you so much, Deena. It broke my heart when you pulled away from me, when we stopped talking to one another. I didn't know what to do. My pride got in the way. And then I got used to the way we related. I forgot how wonderful it had been to hold you, to stroke your hair, to answer all your questions about life. I've missed out on much of our adult relationship. But I don't think that our relationship ends here. Perhaps we'll be closer from now on, even after I've died." I took my mother in my arms, sobbing with relief. The wall had come down. When I sat up again, the room had grown quite dark. The sun had set. Mother's eyes closed as she peacefully drifted into sleep. I kissed her on her forehead and quietly left the room.

When she opened her eyes, Deena was astounded by what had taken place. She had not expected the experience to feel so real. She told me that she felt relieved; expressing what had been bottled up inside and having a meaningful talk with Angela within herself extinguished the urgency she had felt about talking with her mother in the hospital room.

In our next session, Deena had just come from her mother's hospital room. Angela had been comatose, her eyes open but unseeing, and she had been totally unresponsive to Deena's presence. Deena told me that this change in her mother's condition would have been devastating to her if she had not had the internal conversation recounted above. Now she felt comforted not only by that episode but by the thought that she could continue communicating with Angela on this level throughout her dying and after her death.

Talking through the Heart

Many times I talked to my father silently through my heart, a powerful technique I learned from Stephen Levine, author of *Who Dies?* Levine has observed that agitated people are able to quiet down and those in a coma can soften when the person next to them sends love and understanding through the heart. During such transmissions, it is not words that are important but the acceptance and care generated from within.

Levine stresses the discrimination we should use in talking through the heart, taking care not to impose our own needs, desires, or agendas on the dying person—even when we are *sure* we know what's best for that individual. He illustrates this point in *Who Dies?* with this story:

A nurse, after learning from Levine the technique of talking through the heart, tried it with a difficult patient who refused to acknowledge that he was dying. A few times a day she would go into his room and talk silently to him through her heart about how he should accept death, not deny it. Finally, the head nurse told her the patient had requested that she not go into his room anymore. When the nurse asked why, the head nurse responded, "He said you talk too much."

Talking silently through the heart can work at a distance as well as at a bedside. Sonja was caught up in a family drama which involved not telling her father that he was dying of cancer. Unfortunately, in maintaining this secret, she felt she could talk to him only on a superficial level, which was very painful when there was so much more she wanted to discuss. I suggested she try talking to him through her heart, even though he was thousands of miles away. Sonja was doubtful that this could have any effect but tried it anyway. She told her father that she knew he had cancer, that she wanted him to live, but that she was willing to let him go if that was best for him.

After a few weeks, Sonja felt calmer and more at peace with the situation. Then she had a dream in which her father told her, "I know what the doctors won't tell me. I'm all right, so don't worry about me. Remember to put oil in your car and get your tires changed every thirty thousand miles." With this message, Sonja realized that she no longer needed to obsess about her father; rather, she needed to focus on the basic mechanics of living her own life. When she visited him in the hospital shortly thereafter, she was the only family member who was able to sit quietly with him and accept his situation with grace.

Exercise 2-2
CONNECTING THROUGH YOUR HEART WITH A DYING LOVED ONE

Sit down and close your eyes. For a few minutes, bring your full attention to the pattern of your breathing. Feel the breath passing through your nostrils. Then focus on the heart center on the sternum between your breasts. Be aware of any sensations there, no matter how subtle they may be. You may want to touch that area with your fingers. Once your attention is centered there, breathe in and out of your heart.

Now begin to talk to your loved one through your heart—silently, gently, truthfully, compassionately. Let the words flow through your heart on the waves of your breath. You may want to say that you are fully present, that you care, that you want to support the person in the passage, that you will miss the person when death occurs. Or you might simply send love through your heart. Maintain the physical connection with the heart as you silently speak.

Communicating with a Comatose Person

There comes a time when a dying person slips into a dreamless state and is no longer responsive to other people or to the environment. Then communication as we have known it is no longer possible, but internal communication techniques, including talking through the heart, can serve to maintain a connection. If you have been practicing these techniques throughout a loved one's illness, you will not feel as cut off when coma occurs. Internally, you will experience a bridge of communication.

In his brilliant book *Coma*, psychiatrist Arnold Mindell proposes that many people in comatose states are actually in an altered state of consciousness and that it is possible to reach them if we can learn a more refined way of communicating. Mindell listens and watches carefully, acknowledges when he is confused, asks questions, and validates the person's experience. In this way, Mindell is able to engage in a meaningful dialogue that explores any conflicts the person may be experiencing about dying.

After introducing himself, Mindell sits close to the person in a coma, touching the person's wrist or hand, and pacing his own breathing with that of the patient. He next affirms the internal experience of the comatose person, commenting on events that are not apparent to the observer: "Whatever is happening, whatever it is, will show us the way. It is going to be our guide. So continue to feel, see, hear, and move with the feelings, visions, sounds, and movements happening within you. This will bring you wherever we have to go" (Mindell, p. 30). Mindell then looks for subtle cues of response such as spasms, twitches, facial movements, the opening or focusing of the eyes, and changes in the person's breathing. In this way communication is established. Mindell maintains that he has "not met anyone who has not responded to [this] kind of interaction."

In *Coma*, he describes an eighty-year-old patient, John, who had been in a semicomatose state for six months. At the point that Mindell was called in, John was intensely agitated, shouting, and groaning. As I mentioned before, dying people who feel they are misunderstood often become agitated, a concept Mindell fully comprehended and affirmed. He sat down next to John and began to breathe and groan along with him. Even though this man had not spoken a complete sentence for months, a dialogue developed. In broken short phrases, John announced that a big ship was coming for him. With Mindell asking questions that reflected a genuine desire to understand what John was experiencing, John revealed that he was not going to take this ship. John became even more agitated at this point, and Mindell sensed that their dialogue was getting close to the heart of some conflict John had about dying. Mindell continued to ask questions that helped John explore this conflict.

John told him that this ship was coming to take him on vacation, but that he had never taken a vacation and felt that he had to go back to work. Mindell encouraged John to explore the ship and report back to him about what he found. John described angels driving the ship. The trip was also free. With this information, Mindell encouraged John to take the vacation—he could come back or continue on if he wanted to. John's last words were: "Yeah. Yeah. Vacation to the Bahamas. Ba . . . haa . . . mas. Yeah. Hmmm. No work." At this point, John fell into a peaceful sleep and died a half hour later.

Mindell is gifted in initiating verbal dialogues with comatose people who had previously seemed incapable of talking. With some patients, however, he must rely on nonverbal communication, watching for cues such as changes in breathing or subtle body movements—for example, in the mouth, eyes, eyebrows, or hands. If any such movements occur consistently in response to a stimulus, they could suggest a means of communication. One comatose client made only slight eyebrow movements in response to Mindell's statements, but these were enough to enable Mindell to comprehend the person's messages.

The dialogue with John demonstrates the symbolic nature of communication with the dying. Crossing a river or going on a journey are metaphors often used by the dying to describe their experience of crossing over. In *On Dreams and Death*, Marie-Louise Von Franz writes, "In my experience the image of the journey in dreams is also the most frequently occurring symbol of impending death" (Von Franz, p. 64). For John, dying was a journey—and a deeply disturbing prospect, since he had never taken a vacation from work.

Malby, a seventy-year-old man, also had conflicts about dying. Three days before he fell and sustained a fatal injury to the head, he had a vivid dream that he promptly shared with his daughter, Kathleen: "I went across the Rio Grande looking for Ruth. I couldn't find her so I came back." Ruth was his ex-wife; they had been divorced for more than thirty years with little communication. However, when Ruth was dying of bone cancer, Malby became very concerned and wanted to visit her. It was just before the trip was arranged that he fell and hit his head, causing severe hemorrhage to his brain. His statement suggested that he may have wanted to meet his ex-wife in death. He was the first to venture over the Rio Grande, but she was not ready to meet him, so Malby didn't die immediately, as was expected by the doctors. He slipped into a coma that lasted five days.

Realizing Malby's conflict, Kathleen talked to him while he was comatose, assuring him that many other deceased loved ones would be there for him and that Ruth would be meeting him soon. Malby died peacefully, followed two days later by Ruth. This story reminded me of how significant a past relationship can become to the dying—even one that has seemingly faded in outward importance over the years. Kathleen had the sensitivity to listen to Malby without making judgments about what *she* thought was important. Knowing her parents' history of divorce and animosity, she could have easily dismissed Malby's statement about looking for Ruth. However, though she didn't really understand, she was willing to listen to and support her father in his quest to meet Ruth again.

In a deeply moving and now well-known example, Isabel Allende's daughter became ill and then fell into a coma. Certain that Paula would eventually awaken, her mother sought to maintain communication with her daughter by writing a long letter, published as Allende's memoir *Paula*. "Listen, Paula," the book begins. "I am going to tell you a story, so that when you wake up you will not feel so lost." With sensitivity and humor, Allende records the family history and expresses her own fears and emotions as she cares for her unresponsive daughter. Months later she has a vision/dream in which her daughter speaks to her:

> Listen, Mama, wake up. I don't want you to think you're dreaming. I've come to ask for your help. . . . I want to die and I can't. I see a radiant path before me, but I can't take that first step, something is holding me. All that's left in my bed is my suffering body, degenerating by the day; I perish for thirst and cry out for peace, but no one hears me. I am so tired! . . . The only thing holding me back a little is having to go alone; if you took my hand it would be easier to cross to the other side—the infinite loneliness of death frightens me. Help me one more time, Mama. You've fought like a lioness to save me, but reality is overpowering you. It's all useless now. . . . I have lived my time and I want to say good-bye. . . . After I die, we will stay in contact that way you do with your grandparents and Granny; I will be in you as a constant, soft presence, I will come when you call, communication will be easier when you don't have the misery of my sick body before you and you can see me as I was in the good days (Allende, p. 315).

This vision/dream was a turning point for Allende. She realized that her daughter was not going to wake up and that she now needed to help her die rather than fight for her life. Almost a year after becoming comatose, Paula died in her mother's arms "with the same perfect grace that characterized all the acts of her life" (Allende, p. 325). Writing the letter sustained Allende throughout the devastating months of her daughter's coma and prepared her for her daughter's death.

As we gain more understanding of what a comatose person is experiencing, we are less likely to treat this person as though he or she is "not there." It has been a common practice in hospitals to talk insensitively around comatose people, on the assumption that they can hear nothing. Yet many stories are recounted in the near-death literature of those who have awakened from a coma and given detailed accounts of doctors' conversations and procedures.

A client, Jason, shared an unnerving experience he had had in the hospital with his comatose father, Ben. One afternoon, a nurse checked on Ben's vital signs and then proclaimed to Jason in Ben's presence that Ben was in the final stages of dying and probably would not last past midnight. No sooner had the words left her mouth than Ben bolted upright, glared at the nurse, and then sank back down into the bed. As though to spite the nurse, he held on past midnight and passed away the next afternoon.

When you feel that communication has broken down with a person in a coma, try to follow the suggestions of Arnold Mindell. In addition, write your loved one a letter (chapter 4 returns to this idea in more detail) or use exercises 2-1 and 2-2 from this chapter. All these methods will help you maintain a connection with the person who appears to be "unresponsive."

When Death Occurs in Your Absence

Some of my clients' deepest regrets stem from being absent at the moment of their loved one's death. They feel that they have missed the opportunity to say good-bye, express love, and spend those last irreplaceable moments together. Some people simply take a short break from the bedside, only to find that the person has died while they were gone. Some are en route to the hospital and arrive too late. Others have no warning because the person died suddenly. These absences inspire an array of feelings: anger, guilt, regret, sadness, or a combination of these. Particularly where the death is violent or results from suicide or an accident, those left behind can suffer profound emotional distress as they go over and over the details of their last encounter with the deceased and picture possible scenarios of what the dying person experienced.

The same techniques that foster communication can help you place yourself at the scene of your loved one's death. And if you are uncomfortable about where the death took place, you can choose another, more soothing environment. Again, as with previous exercises involving imagery, it is important to experience this place with all your senses. In your imagination, sit with the person who is dying. Express what is in your heart; say good-bye. Be open to any last words your loved one may want to communicate to you, and remember to say, "I love you." Exercise 2-3 will help you use your imagination to experience in detail the passing of a loved one who has died in your absence.

Exercise 2-3
IMAGINING A LOVED ONE'S PASSING

In your sanctuary, sit down and close your eyes. Let go of all distractions and concerns and bring your full attention to the internal landscape of your imagination. Imagine that you are sitting beside the person who is dying. What do you see? Smell? Hear? What are you feeling? Be aware of the sound of the person's breathing. Is it smooth or labored? Light or heavy? Synchronize your breathing to his or her breathing so that you are breathing in and out together.

You are participating in a sacred time of transition, sharing the last moments of a life. Now is the time to express your love, whether through words or touch. Are there any unresolved issues you want to bring up? Listen carefully. Does the person want to speak to you? Explore any resistance you feel about letting go of this person, but since letting go may take days, weeks, or months, don't worry about completing this process before going on to the next part of the exercise.

When you are ready, reassure the person that he or she can move on now. Say good-bye. Be fully present and aware of the last breath. This marks the end of a lifetime and the end of your relationship as you have known it. After death has occurred, take time to sit with the body, reflecting on what has just happened and on your loss. Allow yourself to fully experience the impact; cry if you need to. Now that you have participated fully in your loved one's passing, contemplate your own feelings. Notice any subtle changes in the person's body as time passes. You might also become aware of the presence of their spirit in the room.

When you feel ready, prepare to leave. Open your eyes and record what you have experienced.

Regret and Guilt

Christina was very disappointed that she was not at her mother's side when she died, and she could not stop feeling miserable that her mother, Bette, had died alone. During one of our sessions, I guided her via her imagination to the hospital where Bette had died. Sitting beside the frail body, Christina took Bette's hand. It was cold and slightly stiff, but Christina could feel an almost imperceptible squeeze. Weeping, she told Bette how much she loved her.

As Christina reassuringly held her mother's hand, her mother's breaths grew shorter and more labored. Suddenly she opened her eyes and looked at Christina with indescribable love. Just as quickly, Bette's eyes closed again, and with one more breath, she died with a slight smile on her cracked lips. Christina sobbed, deeply moved that she had shared such a sacred and intimate moment with her mother. She no longer felt the regret that had afflicted her grief.

Suzanne, who was also absent when her mother died, felt a need to explore the questions and regrets she was left with in her grief. She felt guilty about putting her mother in a care home and had questions about what her mother experienced in the hospital during her final days and as she died. In her journal, she wrote, "I'd like to be able to talk with my mother, to ask her the questions I failed to ask during her life and to be present with her now to make up for the times I failed to be present with her in the past. . . . I plan to hold a dialogue with my mother and to use my imagination and my love to hear her answers."

Here is Suzanne's recording of that internal dialogue:

Suzanne: Are you at peace, Mother?

Mother: Yes. But it's not the peace as you think of it. It's not calm passiveness. It's more acceptance and understanding.

Suzanne: I always feel guilty that I did not have you come live with us after Daddy's death. It was so complicated. I thought we had lots of years. I wanted you to be fixed up in the care home near me, and I wanted you to become independent. I had the idea you could enjoy life now that Daddy wasn't there to dominate you. I had plans for us to go on a cruise in the summer. Also, I was afraid of losing my independence if we lived together. It had been so hard-won. When I imagined living with both you and Michael, I didn't see any room for me in the picture. I wondered how I could possibly meet both of your expectations, especially since they would probably be at odds. Was I terribly selfish?

Mother: I didn't understand, it's true. But we can only do what we can do at that time. I didn't hold it against you. I thanked God that I had you. What would I have done, and who would I have turned to, if you had not been there?

Suzanne: How did you feel before you collapsed and were rushed to the hospital from the nursing home the last time?

Mother: I felt alone. I was depressed and discouraged. I couldn't understand how I had ended up there. I wanted to hold onto you, and I was angry—angry at my helplessness and my confusion. No one who worked there seemed to care. A little bit of kindness was the most valuable prize in the world then. I didn't want to burden you. I knew you had your life and your work. I just wanted you to hold me one more time. I wanted something familiar; I wanted to go home.

Suzanne: Did you think of death?

Mother: Yes. "Home" was the key. I began to think of that time I had that experience in the hospital a long time ago.

Suzanne: The near-death experience.

Mother: Yes. I wasn't afraid. And I remembered the way I felt— at peace. I decided that was going to be home for me now. That was the home I could get to. And I imagined your father on the other side. Waiting for me. I waited a long time to have you. I couldn't imagine your not being with me.

Suzanne: Were you angry when you realized they had resuscitated you in the hospital? Were you aware or conscious at all during those nine days on life support?

Mother: I never wanted that to happen. But I died as I had lived, didn't I? Under a doctor's care. I knew you were with me every day. I knew you were there. I went in and out of consciousness. It was painful, but if it hadn't been that way we would never have had that time. And that time was precious to me. It really was. I felt your love with me. When you left to go home for dinner that last day I knew my time was up; I knew I would never see you again. I treasure the time we did have.

Suzanne: I felt a sadness, a resistance from you, when I said good-bye. I assured you I would be back after dinner. I focused on that, because I didn't want to acknowledge to myself that anything other could be the case. You had so much care in the intensive unit. I was angry when they moved you to a regular floor. You didn't have the attention and care you should have had.

Mother: No, I didn't. No one seemed to care; I was just another body to bother with.

Suzanne: When I came into the room after the call to come to the hospital, your body was just lying on the bed. No one had covered you. No one was there to tell me before I entered the room that you had died. I'm so glad Michael was with me. When I saw your body I said to Michael, "She's gone." And that is what it looked like to me. Your body didn't look like my mother. It was obvious to me that you weren't there anymore, that you'd gone.

Mother: I had gone, and it was with relief. But it was not without pain. The pain of separation more than physical pain. But it was, and I knew it was, the way it must be. Except for you, everyone who ever meant anything to me was dead. I did not go fearfully, but rather gratefully, to be with those I loved and to leave you to carry on your life. It was as it should have been. You don't need to have regrets. I loved you in holding on, and I love you in release. Live your life and live in love.

In reading over this dialogue, Suzanne felt very much in communication with her mother. She could feel her mother's presence and love, and her mother's words were consoling and validating. While she felt relieved in expressing the guilt, conflicts, and concerns she had experienced throughout her mother's illness, Suzanne also gained more understanding of what her mother was experiencing while she was dying—the shame, frustrations, fears, and peace.

Using internal communication, we can discover that death need not cut us off from those we love. By writing letters or dialogues like Suzanne's, or simply by talking through our hearts or working with imagery, we can find new potential for change and growth in our relationships with those who are dying and those who have died.

And here's another bonus, too often unrecognized even by those who benefit from it: Any breakthroughs or healing we experience with those who have died can enhance our capacity for meaningful and fulfilling relationships with those who are alive.

3

Dreaming of One Who Has Died

*It is in dreams that the pure sacred life is entered and direct relations
with the gods, spirits and ancestral souls are re-established.*
Mircea Eliade

It is in our dreams that many of us first experience an ongoing relationship with a loved one who has died. As we grieve, it is common to dream vividly of the person, and these dreams can shock us in how real they feel. In the first moments of awakening from such a dream, we are often confused and disoriented, wondering if the person really *is* still alive after all. And then, as we shift to waking consciousness, we realize that indeed this person has died. But the experience of having been with the person in a dream can comfort and reassure us with the knowledge that, in spite of our loss, he or she still lives on within us. Many people treasure these dreams, remembering them for the rest of their lives, and they look forward to the appearance of loved ones in future dreams.

Such after-death dreams fall into several categories:

- Dreams which reassure the dreamer that, although death has occurred, the deceased is still accessible and is not suffering
- Dreams which demonstrate that the relationship with the dreamer has changed but not ended
- Dreams in which unresolved issues in the relationship either arise or are actively addressed
- Dreams in which the deceased gives the dreamer support or guidance

Dreams of Reassurance

Dreams of reassurance can be a great relief to those who are grieving. Often the deceased demonstrates peacefulness and urges the dreamer not to worry. Interestingly, in most dreams it's the *dreamer* who has the greatest difficulty in adjusting to the death that has occurred, not the person who has died. As an example, after her father's death, Beth had this dream:

> In the most vivid dream of my life I was walking with my father. I told him how upset I was that he had died and how good it was to see him again. He turned to me and, with a deep belly laugh, said, "But why are you upset? It's OK with me." I was relieved but told him that I was sad he wasn't with me anymore. He stopped walking, looked into my eyes and said, "Bethy, of course I'm with you."

Shortly after her grandmother's death, Laura dreamed that her grandmother walked into the living room. Laura was comforted to see her again, but confused, too, because she knew that her grandmother had just died. Laura spoke, "I'm so overjoyed to see you again, but I thought that you had died." Her grandmother simply but firmly stated, "I never died." Laura awakened with the certainty that her relationship with her grand-mother had not been severed by death.

Dreams That Confirm a Relationship

Many dreams confirm the fact that the connection with a loved one remains unsevered and that the relationship continues to unfold despite the death of the body. Dreams can show death to have had a transforming effect on both the relationship and the person who has died. As though to emphasize the changes since death, the recently deceased often appear healthy, vital, and younger than when last seen in life.

Adrian sent me a dream she had had a year after her mother's death. For eleven years her mother had been paralyzed and unable to walk, speak, read, or write, even though her mind remained clear. Caring for her mother trapped in a crippled body had been a heartbreaking experience for Adrian.

> I see a large room with people seated in chairs near the walls, leaving the center free. I notice a woman walking briskly around the room, swinging her arms. She is wearing a long loose dress, something like a nightgown. Then I recognize her—my mother! She looks directly at me, smiles, and waves.

Adrian considered this dream a message from her mother, communicating that she was now free of all physical limitations. When Adrian saw the radiant smile and friendly wave, she knew her mother was happy. Even years later, thinking about this dream gave Adrian a sense of deep and comforting joy.

Flo also experienced a dramatic change in her parents via her dreams. Soon after her father's death, he appeared in two dreams in which his robust and youthful body radiated a bright white light. Flo was stunned by this transformation, since her father had been sick for most of her life. After these dreams, Flo felt confident that her father was not suffering in his after-death state. Ten years later, Flo's mother died after months of agonizing medical complications caused by failed heart surgery. After her death, Flo's mother appeared repeatedly in Flo's dreams:

> My mom and I were so close we were just like sisters. We shared everything. She was a very giving, loving, sharing, nurturing kind of person. I wasn't really young when she died, but her death was still traumatic: a long process of dying which transpired over two and a half months of intensive care.

After Mom died, I was convinced that she was going to appear to me and that I wouldn't be able to handle it. I just kept praying that she would come to me in my dreams, and that's what she did.

She was so different: she appeared as my teacher. I recognized her physically, but I didn't recognize her energy; it was completely different from what I had known. She would not allow me to refer to her as "my mother" or say that she was dead; if I did, she would disappear.

She was teaching me that in the afterlife she no longer identified herself as my mother; she had moved on and our relationship had changed. I felt a sense of freedom after these dreams. I knew that she had truly found herself because she had gone beyond what she was able to do in this lifetime—to put herself first at the risk of disappointing someone else. She was teaching me to accept myself *and* her. This made me aware of the ways I was limiting myself in my work, and in certain aspects of my relationships.

At first Flo was disappointed in these dreams, for she missed the warm relationship she had known with her mother. But in the dreams Flo's mother appeared in a way that encouraged Flo to take more risks in her own life and to have the courage to follow her heart.

Author Beth Witrogen McLeod buried both her parents in the same year. When she visited her parents' condo for the last time, she discovered two cardinals, male and female, singing on the deck. Although she had never seen cardinals at the condo before, she thought of her parents immediately since these were her parents favorite birds. The synchronicity was confirmed for her by a dream in which her father kept repeating a phrase, "The red cardinal only comes out in the winter." Beth cried out, "So it *was* you at the condo!" to which her parents replied, laughing "Yes, yes."

Dreams of Unresolved Issues

In his memoir *Patrimony*, Philip Roth describes his decision to bury his father in a shroud, even though he knew that this would be out of character for his father. His father was not an Orthodox Jew but rather a "sturdy man rooted all his life in everydayness." Six weeks after the burial, Roth dreamed that his father appeared in a white shroud, admonishing him, "I should have been dressed in a suit. You did the wrong thing" (Roth, p. 237).

It is very common for unresolved feelings to surface in dreams soon after a death, especially insights that were too frightening or threatening to face when the person was still alive. Personality flaws or weaknesses, family secrets, alcoholism, drug addiction, incidents of incest—all such repressed material may come to light.

In *Bradshaw On: The Family*, John Bradshaw refers to the family trance, an unquestioned view of reality shared by the members of a family. Bradshaw shows how this trance is broken by "leaving home, growing up, breaking the bond with Mother." This trance can also be shattered when a family member, particularly a parent, dies. It is then that we can begin to recognize the constrictive conditioning we grew up with and gain insight into issues we may have previously overlooked.

Our dreams inform us of the presence of these unaddressed issues and offer guidance into healing. When we ignore such dreams, they often repeat themselves—and if we continue to ignore them, they can develop into nightmares. Gale reported having persistent nightmares of the dying of her father, who had passed away when Gale was an adolescent. Gale awakened upset from these dreams, unable to shake off the images of her father's suffering. She had not grieved when he died or since—and had never believed that she needed to. But the nightmares signaled the presence of her unresolved grief at a time when she could face it in therapy. As Gale began to grieve actively, her dreams gave her images of a father increasingly healthy. The more she healed, the healthier he became. Finally, when this phase of grieving had been completed, her father stopped appearing. However, note that I said this *phase* of grieving: We are never completely over grief, and it is normal for it to resurface from time to time. I cautioned Gale to expect her father to appear again in future dreams, most likely at times when her grief became active once more.

In another example, soon after Paul's mother's death, he had repeated dreams in which his mother appeared drunk, staggering about the room and slurring her words. These dreams drove home the fact that she had indeed been alcoholic, a problem that the family had avoided facing when she was alive.

When all the family members are alive, the family system is carefully held in place. When one of the members dies, the system is thrown into a chaotic state, destabilizing each family member. Old ways of coping are no longer effective; those left behind feel exhausted, losing their enthusiasm for living. This exhaustion combined with a sense of disorientation and disillusionment make room for new awarenesses to break into consciousness—awarenesses that at other times a person could keep at bay.

In his grief, Paul could no longer sustain his denial of his mother's alcoholism; through his dreams he could see it clearly. At first he felt overwhelmed by this new awareness and resisted letting go of the more comforting image of his mother. However, in his grief support group, Paul was relieved to hear that others also had had disturbing insights after a family member's death. With the support and encouragement of the group members, he learned to talk about his inner turmoil and to educate himself about adult children of alcoholics.

Conversely, some dreams may bring home the painful knowledge that the dreamer failed to appreciate or honor the positive qualities of the person who died. A client named Tom reported in a session that he hadn't liked his brother, Robert, very much when he was alive. Tom felt so tense after each visit that he avoided contact with his brother as much as possible. After one lengthy separation, his brother died suddenly of a heart attack. Though devastated, Tom was relieved when Robert appeared in a dream a few weeks after his death. He stood silently before Tom, smiling broadly, his eyes fixed on Tom in a loving gaze. Ecstatic at seeing his brother, Tom felt overcome with a deep love for him. In the dream, he suddenly realized how sincere and caring his brother had been, qualities he had never noticed when his brother was alive. After the dream, Tom continued to explore this new relationship through imagery exercises.

A dramatic dream opened the way for a woman I will name Rose to appreciate and honor her father in a way that had been impossible when he was alive—because she hadn't known that he was her father. In the months before this man died, Rose had learned some startling information about her mother and had just begun to explore the possibility that a close family friend was actually her father. She had intended to have a talk with him about this, for she felt confident that he knew the truth. However, he died before this talk could take place. Shortly thereafter, Rose had a significant dream in which she held this man in her arms as he was dying. He looked up at her tenderly. "My darling daughter," he said. "So you really believe I am your daughter?" Rose asked. "Of course," he replied. Knowing that in the dream her father was going to die in her arms, Rose awakened in a state of profound joy and peace.

Dreams can also highlight what is being repressed in the grieving process. Joseph dreamed about his wife, Lynne, a few months after her death. In the dream, Lynne was stretched out on a bed, looking very pale and weak. With great effort, she held out her hand to her husband. The tenderness of that gesture touched him so deeply that he awakened from the dream sobbing. The tears surprised him, for he had tried to maintain composure since his wife's death. But this dream had broken through his defenses, and now it felt good to let down and weep. Weeks later his wife appeared again in a dream; this time she was healthy and contented.

Dreams of Support or Guidance

Many people who are grieving have dreams in which the deceased gives them support or guidance. In fact, sometimes the person seems more compassionate and insightful in death than in life.

In an interview, novelist Oscar Hijuelos described how his deceased father helped him through a particularly stressful period of his life. While working on his novel *The Mambo Kings*, Hijuelos broke into a painful rash that seriously interfered with his writing. He felt that this rash erupted out of his guilt over exposing family secrets in his book. At the height of his crisis, Hijuelos had a dream in which his father tenderly washed him in a river. When he awakened, he had a strong sense of well-being, and the rash was gone. Hijuelos felt convinced that his father had given him his blessing to go ahead and write the book.

In chapter 1, I referenced Doreen's dream about her father shortly after his death. In this dream, the family were gathered around her father. Her brothers and sisters were firing questions at him about the estate. The father, who in life had successfully managed and controlled the family money, was clearly annoyed by these questions and told the family, "These things don't concern me now." He then turned to Doreen, who was standing in the back of the room, and assured her in a soft but firm voice, "I've seen to it that your crops will not fail." Doreen was very moved by this dream, both by the dramatic change in her father's values and by his reassurance about her "crops." She felt perplexed by this statement but interpreted it to mean that her father was looking after her and that she would be able to provide well for herself. Many people report dreams in which the deceased loved one expresses a change in values or perspective, as the father in this dream did when he stated, "These things don't concern me now."

Dreams of the Dying

The dreams of the dying can teach us of their conflicts and attempts to prepare for death. Careful attention to dreams may reveal to us unfinished business or fears about death that prevent them from dying in peace. Dream pioneer Marie-Louise Von Franz gives many case histories of clients whose dreams served as preparation for their deaths, but she also suggests that the unconscious itself does not embrace death but behaves as though the individual's psychic life will continue on. The unconscious, she believes, prepares consciousness not for a definite end but for a transformation. In Fraser Boa's *The Way of the Dream*, Von Franz relates the dream of a dying woman in which a candle was slowly burning down on a windowsill. As the candle began to flicker, the woman began to panic, thinking that a great darkness was coming. At that moment, the candle suddenly appeared burning brightly on the sill on the other side of the window. Von Franz interprets this dream to mean, "Yes, the candle of your life is flickering. But life will continue in another medium, in another sphere. Beyond the isolating threshold of the window, that very same life will be going on" (Boa, p. 214).

This dream helped this woman reframe her understanding of death: She learned to see it not as a closed door but as a threshold experience. In nature, thresholds are phenomena that involve sudden changes in the form of matter—for example, the point at which a liquid freezes or a liquid evaporates. Death, writes Von Franz, may be such a threshold, involving a transformation of life as we have known it.

Jeremy's Dream

While there was no current crisis in his life, Jeremy consulted me because his work and personal life felt flat and meaningless. Exhausted most of the time, he no longer felt excited about anything. I encouraged him to bring a dream to therapy. At first, he insisted that he didn't dream. I asked him to set an intention to remember a dream before he went to sleep, to put a pad and pen by his bed, and whenever he woke up, to immediately write down whatever he remembered about a dream, no matter how brief or seemingly insignificant. He brought a disturbing dream to our next session: Sick horses were dying in a dark cellar. Without food, water, or light, some horses had already died. After briefly discussing the dream, I asked him to close his eyes and reenter the dream. In his imagination he went back into the cellar.

When he did, he agonized over the horses' suffering. Surrounded by a stench of decomposing bodies, they huddled helplessly in the darkness. Whereas once they had feasted on golden hay brought by their owners, no one now came to feed or care for them. Suddenly from a dark corner, Jeremy's mother stepped forward. She did not speak but tenderly extended her pale hand toward him.

When Jeremy opened his eyes again, we discussed what he had experienced. He was surprised by how easily he had been able to slip back into the dream. The horses had appeared as vividly as they had in his original dream. But he was perplexed by the appearance of his mother, which had not taken place in his dream.

His voice cracking and his face flushed with emotion, Jeremy spoke of his mother, who had died when he was five, leaving his father to struggle financially and the extended family to help as it could. Up to this point in psychotherapy, Jeremy had minimized the impact on him of this traumatic event from his childhood, even though his mother had been an attentive, loving, nurturing presence. It occurred to Jeremy as he reflected on his dream that as the horses had been abandoned, so had he. And as the horses were suffering, so was he. While Jeremy had not dreamed initially about his mother, the images of the decaying and dying horses were disturbing enough to bring the loss of her to consciousness. Immersing himself in the dream again through his imagination, he was able to make a connection between the state of the horses and his own unresolved grief. He wondered what would happen if he descended into the dark caverns of his grief and gave it his full attention for a period of time. Would his vitality return?

When he talked about these insights in our next session, we focused on his buried grief, and this led to an outpouring of sadness. In poignant dialogues with his mother, Jeremy told her how helpless and alone he had felt when she died. He wept when his mother shared her deep sorrow in having to leave him and expressed her abiding love for him. In Jeremy's next dream, the horses were gone and the cellar was brightly furnished as a living room. Images of living had replaced the images of dying: Jeremy's unresolved grief was no longer draining the life force out of him.

Preparation Dreams

Dreams often help to prepare a person *before* a loss. For example, a client of mine dreamed that her mother told her, "I'm ready to join your father. Don't worry about me. I'll be fine." My client awakened in a state of profound peace that lasted for weeks. She knew that her mother was ready to die and that she would die soon, and her dream inspired her to spend as much time with her mother as she could during the last days of her life.

Writer Laurens van der Post recalls a dream in which his good friend Carl Jung stood at the garden gate, waving his hand and calling out to him, "I'll be seeing you." Jung died that night. Such dreams of an anticipated death can prepare and comfort a person, for they suggest that, even as we are on the brink of losing someone we love, a link with that person remains within the psyche which will not be broken by death.

While such dreams are readily understandable, others may be more opaque. I had a perplexing dream a year before my father's death. In the dream, I answered a knock on my hotel-room door and my father stood silently, lovingly extending a white chrysanthemum toward me. There was something about this flower that I didn't want to accept, and I tried to close the door. I awakened from the dream feeling very agitated. It was only after the cancer diagnosis that I realized that the chrysanthemum was a funeral flower and that the dream had come to prepare me for my father's death. When I had the dream, no one knew that my father had or would develop cancer, although I now suspect that the cancer was already quietly present in his body. Even though I rejected the message of the dream at the time, I do feel in retrospect that the powerful image of the flower in my father's hand planted a seed in my psyche that would grow in time into an acceptance of my father's terminal diagnosis.

It is probable that many preparation dreams slip by unnoticed. You may awaken disturbed and confused by a dream that makes no sense to you now but that could come to have deep meaning. For this reason, your dream journal can help you keep in touch not just with the dreams you are working with but with past dreams whose relevance may eventually be revealed. Had I not recorded the chrysanthemum dream in my dream journal, I would have forgotten it and would never have made the connection between the flower and my father's illness.

Many people are comforted by preparation dreams, but others may experience them with distress, finding themselves left with a sense of dread, helplessness, or guilt. Jean dreamed that on a visit to the home of her sister, Ann, her sister seemed strangely, disturbingly detached. Suddenly it occurred to Jean that Ann was dead, but as Jean panicked, Ann laughed and counseled her not to worry.

Jean awakened shaking uncontrollably and drenched in sweat. She called Ann immediately and was relieved to hear her voice. However, the dream filled her with dread. Was Ann going to die? Was there anything she could do to prevent it? Afraid that speaking of her dream might make it come true, she pushed it into a dark corner of her psyche, where it festered for five months. Then one evening she received the phone call she had been dreading: Ann had died in a car accident. While Jean acknowledged that the dream *did* help her after her sister's death, she resented the distress she experienced for so many months beforehand.

If you have such a dream, treat it as a wake-up call. If we do not die first, we will witness the death of every one of our loved ones—perhaps soon, perhaps later. If your loved one were to die tomorrow, what would you regret? What would be left unsaid? What issues would be left unresolved? What can you do *today* to feel more at peace with that person and with yourself? Preparation dreams don't have to throw you into a frozen panic; they can mobilize you to act now to bring healing into your relationships.

Dreams as Grief Progresses through Stages

The first response to the death of a loved one is shock or denial. Unable to fully absorb the impact of the death that has just occurred, the mind and body respond with numbness. Edges are blurred, feelings dulled. "I just can't believe it" is a common response. Dreams at this stage may reflect this shock. A number of my clients have dreamed about loved ones being simultaneously alive and dead, reflecting their confusion. For example, Tamara dreamed that her husband was dead on the bed when suddenly the living husband walked into the room. She felt torn between the dead and the living husband. Which should she relate to? Which was real? Others dream about their loved one's being dead and then awaken with the hope that it was all just a bad dream. Or a person may appear vital and healthy in a dream, convincing the dreamer that "He's alive after all! He didn't die." These dreams reflect the shock and denial that predominate throughout this early stage, when a person is struggling to integrate this new information into his or her reality. Shock and denial help to buffer a person from the full impact of the loss, and dreams during this period may perform the same function.

On the other hand, many people in this early stage of grieving do not dream of the deceased at all. Instead, they find themselves searching in their dreams for the person without success. In *Mourning Unlived Lives*, Judith Savage states that searching dreams mostly occur shortly after the death itself and that they often stop when the griever begins to accept the reality of the loss.

Eventually, though, the fact of death hits hard, eliciting powerful and often overwhelming waves of emotions. When this happens, chaotic dreams with dark, even frightening images are common. In this period, many people dream that they are lost or confused. Or they may dream about being swept up in some tidal wave or storm. It helps to understand that these dreams reflect what is taking place in the psyche: a breaking down of old structures and the welling up of primal emotions, both of which can contribute to a sense of being out of control. The loss of a loved one shakes up the very foundation of your life, flooding you with such intense feelings that normal functioning seems impossible. The resulting disorientation can be debilitating, but it can also shatter your limited sense of yourself. If you can surrender to this process of breaking down and dissolving, grief will transform you. You will emerge from it stronger and more vital than you were when you entered it.

Elva, who lost her father in her college years, had repeated dreams of being lost on dark streets and searching through dark houses. After her father's death, she felt utterly lost and depressed. She told me that her dreams comforted her by reflecting so accurately in images what she was experiencing emotionally. They also guided her quite explicitly toward the inner work that she needed to do in her grief. In one dream she asked a man if she could explore his house, for she had heard that it had many secret passageways. After a long silence, the man told her that she had her own house now. Elva argued with him. "But I want to explore your house because of its secret passages," she said. "Your house has secret passages too," came the reply. "No, it doesn't," insisted Elva. "Yes, the secret passages are there." "Where?" "In the closets." "But I've looked in all the closets." "The passages are there. You have to clean out the closets first."

Elva realized that if she cleaned out her psychic closets, discarding what she could no longer use, she would have access to something new. She was excited about where the secret passages might lead. Alongside the dark images in her dreams there were whispers of confirmation that she was progressing through her grief and not just stuck in her depression as she had feared.

During the first year after my own father's death, I had a series of dreams that my house was being remodeled, room by room. Starting with the foundation, each room had to be torn apart in order to be rebuilt. It was hard for me to visualize the outcome in the midst of this remodeling, that the violent tearing down of walls and breaking of windows could ultimately create a more spacious and livable room. Indeed, my father's death did tear apart the world I had known, and as I shared my grief with friends and family, many walls came down, generating more vulnerability and intimacy in my relationships.

One of the dangers during deep grief is that the person will hold on to grief, even when the psyche is ready to let it end. Although it is more likely for people to wrench themselves prematurely out of their grief, some do hold on to it and refuse to reenter the arena of daily life. If this goes on for too long, it is not uncommon for a deceased loved one to appear in dreams and encourage or admonish the dreamer to go on with life. After his mother's death, a man wrote me that his deceased brother appeared to him in a dream and told him, "It is not your time yet, so live. But when it is time, bring a sweater, for it's cold."

Throughout the long active phase of grief, dreams about the deceased loved one are reassuring. These dreams demonstrate that an ongoing relationship exists, even though it is common during this time to doubt this. Ronald had a dream about his wife, Linda, six months after she died. Since he had not dreamed about her since her death, he was overjoyed to see her. As they talked and visited, he told her that he had doubted that the relationship with her would continue after her death. He thought that she would no longer be involved with him or his life. Linda was angry to hear that he had had so little faith, and she lovingly chastised him. In the dream he realized that without a doubt she was present within him.

Dreams can sometimes take you through a loved one's dying even years after the event. Most often, such dreams occur early in the grieving process, but in fact they can occur at any time. If you do find yourself reliving a loved one's death in your dreams, and if you find these episodes disturbing and/or repetitive, it can be useful to perform exercise 2-3, "Imagining a Loved One's Passing," in chapter 2.

Dreams often change in content as we move out of grief and into acceptance of the death, challenging us to live with a greater sense of aliveness and authenticity. Changes in self-concept, values, career and work, relationships, and religious and spiritual beliefs that have been developing below the surface throughout grief now begin to manifest outwardly. This is a time ripe with ideas, creativity, and potential, a time of expansion, stretching, and thinking big. Dreams at this stage suggest new possibilities, directions, and hopes. They thus reflect excitement about coming changes as well as any resistance, hesitation, and doubts that may surface in response.

Elva, who had dreamed about the dark streets for so many months, experienced a change in her dreams in the weeks leading up to the first anniversary of her father's death. In one dream, a small coffin sat on the altar in a church. On the coffin was written, "A new life is born today." She also dreamed that she was marrying herself in a Hindu ceremony. Elva attributed this dream to changes in her self-esteem that she had experienced since her father's death. She felt much more loving and accepting of herself and more confident in her capacity to confront challenging situations. Again, close to the first anniversary of her parent's death, another client dreamed that she was climbing a tall ladder and, just as she reached the top rungs of the ladder, was helped over the top by a woman who gave her a boost from behind.

Often dreams at the end of grief reflect changes in the inner relationship with a deceased loved one. By this time you might be trusting that the relationship will continue and no longer will need to be confirmed through repeated dreams as was necessary earlier. You may come to expect long periods in which a loved one does not appear in your dreams at all. But you could find yourself savoring occasional dream visits. Elva anguished that she did not dream about her father until close to a year after his death. When finally he did appear, he was annoyed that she didn't trust that he had been with her all the while. To him there had been no break in their relationship. Months after the first anniversary of her father's death, Elva had a dream in which she had a date with her father in a lovely old hotel. She dressed up, bought two glasses of wine (a full-bodied cabernet for her father, a rosy zinfandel for herself), and went downstairs to meet him. He was healthy and slim, as he had been in younger days. They were both overjoyed and toasted one another.

Her relationship with her father continued to unfold. Five years after his death she had this dream:

> It was All Soul's Day, the day before my twenty-fourth birthday. Exhausted from a bad bout of insomnia I had suffered the previous night, I left work early and went home to take a nap. As I drifted deep into sleep, my father appeared, looking robust and sturdy, the way he had the day his doctor sat him in a leather office chair and told him he had one year to live. Now he was visiting me at my place of work, as if to survey the life I had made for myself here in San Francisco. I greeted him in the reception area and took him by the hand, leading him down the hallway to my desk. When he got there, I sat him down and gave him something to eat. I was surprised to see him pick the food up with his hands, missing his mouth several times as he tried to take it in. As I wiped his chin and fingers with a napkin, I realized that he had forgotten how to live in the body, how to navigate the small necessities of earthly life.
>
> For a moment I felt sad, seeing him sit there so awkward in his flesh, knowing this would be the last time he would visit me in this outgrown form. But before my tears could come, he stood up, took me by the hand, and led me back down the hallway and out

of the building. As we made our way outside, he began to sing. Soon I was singing with him, our voices rising and falling in gentle harmony, until, finally, he sang the last note and let go of me.

A moving dream that clearly demonstrates a beloved's dream visit in the emergence phase is described in Paul Eppinger's book *Restless Mind, Quiet Thoughts*. Over a year after Paul's suicide, his father, who published Paul's journals posthumously, had a dream that he and his son were hiking together in the mountains. Walking along in silence for a time, his son appeared content and healthy. He then told his father,

> "Dad, all of my earlier confusion and despair has lifted. It's so much better for me here; I can see clearly that the world just wasn't really suited for me. Strange how we humans have drifted, generation after generation, further and further from any natural kind of life. . . . If I could only have trusted my self—my insides— just a little more back then, I might have made it. . . . Now, I'm going to take the steeper trail to the right, if you continue to the left, there's a great view just ahead up there. So my journey continues—and so does yours. We'll talk again the next time we meet. Until then, adios" (Eppinger, p. 195).

Paul and his father met in this dream as they would have in life. They shared silence and words and then parted, each taking a different path. There was the assumption that in time they will meet again—perhaps in another dream.

Thus, your dreams are precious gifts that will guide you through the challenges of grief and remind you that in the imagination you have not lost contact with those who have died. Your dreams will let you know if you are suppressing your grief and will inform you of what you need to attend to in order to heal. They will change in response to shifts in your grieving.

Initial dreams often reflect the shock and denial that the griever is experiencing. Dreams throughout the most active phase of grief may be chaotic, even frightening. After many months of intense grieving, your dreams may encourage you to expand, engage in new possibilities, and explore new directions. Trust the wisdom of your dreams; they connect you to the vast imaginative realm of the unconscious where resources for deepening and healing from loss abound. The following steps will help you retrieve and work with your dreams.

Seven Steps for Working with Dreams

1. The first step is to establish a relationship with your dreams as messengers from the unconscious. Perhaps you have always ignored your dreams or devalued the messages from this part of your psyche. But most cultures of the world have used dreams as healing tools, and Freud and Jung, the great genius/explorers in the mapping of the human psyche, proved the great value that dreams have for us as conduits to instinct, buried memories, and the unconscious. If you have avoided this area of your reality, you may have to convince the unconscious that you do value its feedback and that now you are willing to listen. If you approach dreams with respect, humility, and receptivity, you will build a constructive relationship with your unconscious.

2. Before you go to sleep, actively decide that you want to remember a dream, that you are open to whatever the unconscious presents to you. If you are currently struggling with a particular problem or issue, ask for a dream that will address it specifically.

Put a pen and paper (or tape recorder) and a flashlight by your bed, and make the commitment to write down whatever fragment or dream that you remember. Then go to sleep. If you awaken in the middle of the night with a dream, write it down immediately. Make brief notes that you can elaborate on later. Many assume that they will remember a dream only to find the next day that it has flown.

In the morning, don't get out of bed or talk to anyone until you have taken some time to reflect on your dreams. Without editing, write down whatever you remember, including fragments. Sometimes a fragment is like the tail of a fish—if you take hold of it firmly, the rest of the dream may follow out of the watery depths. And even if you don't remember the rest of the dream, the fragment itself can often be a rich source of insights.

If you have trouble remembering your dreams, be patient. Don't give up. Some friends and clients have had success with writing on paper or even in the air, "I want to remember a dream tonight." Or you can work with a guided imagery exercise in which you close your eyes, imagine yourself going to sleep and having a dream, and then awakening in the morning with a clear memory of the dream

3. Later, record your dream in a dream journal. Referring to your notes, write the dream in the present tense as though it were unfolding now. Then give it a title. Writing the dream down in a special place gives it importance and sends the message to the unconscious that you are taking its messages seriously.

After you have recorded your dream, take some time to reflect on it. Prepare for the unexpected; admit your ignorance. Approach the dream humbly, setting aside snap judgments. Remember that a dream works on many levels at once; a dream can never be reduced to just one meaning. You may feel baffled, disturbed, and even resistant—all this is natural in working with dreams. Your task at this point is simply to just sit with the dream images and let them work on you. After a lifetime of studying dreams, Carl Jung confessed that they remained a mystery to him. He did not feel confident that his way of working with dreams could be called a method. However, Jung did feel certain that something always came of meditating on a dream, turning it over and over for a period of time.

4. To begin exploring what needs resolution in a dream, ask questions of the dream and of the dream figures. Here are some sample questions to pose to the dream:

- What am I doing or not doing in this dream?
- What are the significant actions in this dream?
- What are the feelings in this dream?
- Who are the dream figures in this dream?
- What are the issues, conflicts, and unresolved situations?
- What possibilities for healing are present?
- What questions does this dream raise for me?
- What images stand out?
- What associations come up for me with each image?
- What is being wounded and/or healed in this dream?
- Does this dream have a relationship to other dreams?
- Do any situations in my daily life come to mind as I reflect on this dream?
- What new choices does this dream suggest or inspire?

Here are some sample questions to ask of the people who appear in your dream:

- What do you want?
- What do you want to show me?
- Do you have any messages for me?
- What is your gift?
- What do I need to do to develop a relationship with you?
- Where do you want to take me?

5. Look for threads connecting this dream with other dreams. If you find yourself dreaming regularly about a similar theme, in your dream journal read carefully over all the dreams in that series. Perhaps an early dream in a series introduces the issues to be explored in subsequent dreams. Or maybe a later dream offers critical information that was missing in earlier ones.

6. As you move through these steps, remember that a dream can never be reduced to just one meaning. If you feel confident about any one interpretation of a dream, stay open to other possibilities as well. Writer/psychologist James Hillman insightfully writes, "If we think back on any dream that has been important to us, as time passes and the more we reflect on it, the more we discover in it, and the more varied the directions that lead out of it. Whatever certainty it once might have given shifts into complexities beyond clear formulations each time the dream is studied anew. The depth of even the simplest image is truly fathomless. This unending, embracing depth is one way dreams show their love" (Hillman, p. 200).

7. Other methods will help you explore your dream further:

- Dialogue with dream figures or images.
- Adopt the persona of the different people, animals, or objects in your dream and reexperience the dream from that perspective.
- Paint or draw the dream; sculpt a dream image.
- Act out your dreams.
- In your imagination, go back into the dream and redream it. The following exercise will show you how to reenter your dream.

Exercise 3-1
REENTERING A DREAM

When you have a dream about one who has died, write it down. Take a few minutes to recall the most significant or vivid part of the dream in which this person appeared. Then, close your eyes and reenter the dream by placing yourself in that environment. Even if you didn't notice any smells, sounds, or textures in your original dream, experience this place now with all your senses. Look around you. Touch, smell, listen. Continue to explore this environment with your senses until you feel fully present in your body. This will help you move from your memory of the dream to an experience of it in the present.

Next, pay close attention to the person's expression, movements, and dress. If the details seem vague, focus, as you might through the lens of a camera, on one small part of that person. As you concentrate on this part, other details may become clearer. Then expand your focus to include the whole person.

It takes time to develop your inner senses; you may not be able to see images clearly the first few times you work with imagery exercises. Even without gleaning any details of the person, you'll be able to sense his or her presence. Be aware of what you are feeling.

To create an opportunity for interaction, approach the person directly. You may want to ask the questions on page 67 as possible queries of your dream figures.

In the following days, look for ways in which you can express the dream images you created when you were asleep. For example, after Elva had her dream about marrying herself in a Hindu ceremony, I encouraged her to create a ritual based on the dream. She enlisted two friends and conducted a ceremony based on vows she had written for herself; these reflected a commitment to a more loving and accepting relationship to herself. Another client who had a powerful dream about a lion felt inspired to buy a shirt with a lion's head painted on it. Wearing this shirt brought out the lion in him—it actually made him feel more courageous and energetic. In this way, a dream is a call to wake up and live more fully.

4

Letters: Beginning a Correspondence

Something has changed for me while writing this letter.
I feel strangely empty yet at the same time more open to my love for you.
You are becoming a part of my life again.
A workshop participant

Give sorrow words; the grief that does not speak
Whispers the oe'r fraught heart, and bids it break.
William Shakespeare

Dreams of deceased loved ones surprise and comfort us. Most people feel such dreams occur too infrequently and are deeply frustrated to lose the connection upon awakening—as if a phone line had suddenly gone dead. They wait and wait for more dreams, believing them to offer the only way to make contact. But you don't *have* to wait. Use the communication methods in this and succeeding chapters to gain access to and explore this unique relationship. You can do the exercises in the order they are presented or simply try the ones you feel most drawn to. But always do retreat to the sanctuary you have established in your home to perform the activity you choose.

Writing a Letter

We begin with a technique for opening a communication that is perhaps the easiest approach, affording the least resistance, even when both parties are living. Writing a letter allows you to reflect, choose, rework, revise, and take as much time as you need to express yourself fully.

Within the terrain of a letter, you have the freedom to express yourself honestly, directly, and completely without worrying about the other person's response. This sort of *carte blanche* will help you express whatever you have held back or silenced in your communication and will thus pinpoint the issues you need to resolve in your relationship. For example, write about what experiences you have been through since your loved one died, what you miss, what you have learned about yourself and the relationship, what you appreciate and resent in your relationship, what you want to carry on. If certain issues have surfaced since the death, or issues have begun to bother you that were never addressed when the person was alive, write about these. If you are bringing up an event from the past that you wish to resolve, you may want to redefine what happened, describing exactly how you felt about it and how you'd like to change it. Write about how this event has affected you and what you want for the present. Remember, you'll find that your communication flows more freely if you avoid blaming, preaching, or demanding. Still, express yourself honestly and authentically, not avoiding or dampening your real feelings, even if they are distressingly negative.

Don't feel discouraged if your first letter is full of anger. It is common to feel angry at your loved one for dying and for causing the hurts and disappointments that people always do effect upon each other to one degree or another. You may need to express uncomfortable feelings, thoughts, and memories before you can move on to feeling more compassionate, loving, or understanding. And it may not be possible to make this shift in one letter; it may take several letters to get to a point of closure. But remember throughout that as soon as you start writing a letter to your loved one, you are initiating a process of healing that will go at its own pace. You can actively participate in this process, but you can't control or force it.

Here are some sample questions you might ask yourself as you write your letter:

- What experiences have I been through since my loved one's death?
- What do I miss?
- What do I regret?
- What issues in our relationship remain unresolved?
- What do I resent?
- What do I appreciate?
- What have I learned about myself, my loved one, and our relationship?
- What do I want to carry on?

Ask yourself the following questions after you have written your letter:

- Was I open and honest?
- Did I express my love and appreciation?
- Did I address unresolved issues in our relationship?
- Do I still feel regrets?
- Are any resentments still bothering me?
- Is anything left unsaid?
- Do I feel forgiveness? Do I feel more understanding?

Marianne's Letter

Marianne wrote this letter to her brother, who had died in an accident while he was attending college in England:

Dearest James,

I ask where you are and in the voices of the rain and the wind I sense you telling me that this is the wrong question, that you *are* but there is no *where*. It's a tentative question I've asked. I realize that I'm resisting talking to you. I don't want to open myself up to the pain again. My throat feels tight and my neck and shoulders are very still. They are capping off my heart's feelings.

I've tried several ways of reaching out to you, but there is no clear imagery, no sound of your voice. It's even hard for me to see your face. What does come up is a stream of pictures, like watching cuts of home movies out of our life together as we grew up. There seems to be no way to stop the stream to look at a single "frame." Our brief life together flows by and disappears—such a brief moment. If only I could wind it back and show you how precious you were to me.

Now the tears come . . . those "if onlys" cause such pain.

I realize how little I have allowed myself to feel my own sorrow in your death. Mum and Dad were so overwhelmed and in such agony that I felt I had to be there for them, to support them. There didn't seem to be anywhere for me to go to grieve for myself. No one in the States knew you, and Mum and Dad actually asked me not to come home for your funeral because they didn't want to add to the pain by having to say good-bye to me afterwards. I didn't know any better then. I didn't have enough self-confidence to override them and do what my heart told me: to go home, to be with them and with you, to see your poor body, to hear the words and songs of your funeral, to cry with Mum and Dad holding your ashes in a little box on my lap, to be in the silence of the mourning house.

One of the hardest things for me is to move beyond the stuckness I feel about what actually happened to you. I know that it was early morning; you were on your way to work. Your van had broken down and you were trying to fix it. Some other people had stopped and, I suppose, were going to try and help you. Then a lorry came by, too fast I imagine, and hit you, and drove on. It's possible that the driver never knew what he had done. I know they never found him; that felt so unfinished for so long.

The other people saw him hit you. At first I tried to imagine the scene over and over again. It's almost as if I was trying to force the reality into my own body so that I could realize what had happened. There are so many unanswered questions: Did you die instantly? What happened to your body? Was it badly damaged? Was there a lot of pain? And in the death itself: Were you free to go or were you caught not knowing whether you were alive or dead?

I know that you were with Mum, for she felt and heard you reassuring her. That helped us all, I think. There's so much that I don't know and still don't feel able to talk about with Mum and Dad. Maybe I don't need to. This is something for me to explore in myself. I need to see if I can just let go or if I have to actually re-create what happened as a way to bring closure.

So, now, after all these years, what do I write to you? I don't even remember the date of your death. October 10th, I think, 1980. The year that Mount Saint Helens exploded. I remember those endless pictures of gray smoke. It was a gray fall, a gray winter. It's hard to pierce through the fog with which I shroud that time.

Sometimes I see you very vividly in my dreams. It feels as if your death was the real dream and that, when I wake up, I can just call you on the phone and we'll be talking and laughing as though no time has passed since we last saw each other.

How little time we really spent together after we both went to boarding school and then to college—our culture didn't really invite passion, did it? Nonetheless, I treasure the sweet loving connection that we made the last few times we saw each other, and I know in my heart that you also cared and loved intensely. My heart still feels pain, not to be able to hold you and express that love through physical presence.

I do believe you are with me in some way. I sometimes think that I can feel you encouraging me as I make all these changes in my life—going to school, creating my wonderful relationship with G., waking up to life in ways that encourage me to move over edges into new places.

Taking this class and writing this letter have pushed me to really pay attention to the sense of your presence. As I write this I can feel a little shift as if I'm releasing my grip on the pain of the memories and allowing myself to make some space for a new relationship to you. A little panic comes up. "But I don't want to forget. The pain helps me remember." And the answer comes: "Let go of the old pain. It prevents you from opening to your deepest creative feelings. There will be sadness and tears, but the passion can only grow if you allow the light to come in. Release your grip. Let go."

James, be with me in my letting go of you. Maybe this sounds a bit crazy, but I know that I'll feel your presence in life more clearly if I release my fear of losing you. I have lost you in the physical realm. You've gone. But I'm beginning to realize the truth of other sorts of presence—in energy, awareness, intensity. I know you're there.

Now, a few days later, I look back over some of what I've written. The first thing that comes up is a kind of wonder at how deeply I still feel love for you. It's so alive, so present. With that feeling comes a little shyness. I know there is so much that I will never learn about you and your life. I know that your friends from Oxford were much closer to you as an adult than I ever was, and there's a part of me that feels almost presumptuous about my sense of intimacy and love.

So much has changed in our family since your death, I think *because* of your death. We are close and attentive now. We treasure our times together and talk from the heart about many things. We are much more loving—openly loving. What a price to pay in order to claim and express our love for each other. And what a commitment, because of that price, to really honor our connection from the heart. In a way, it is the "you" in us which energizes our love for each other.

I'm reluctant to stop writing as if, by doing so, I'll break this feeling of connection with you. But I know now that I can do this. I know that the pain is bearable and that by opening, it lightens and releases you, and me.

So thank you for being with me. Thank you for your loving soul.

Like so many who have written letters to deceased loved ones, Marianne experienced significant shifts in her grief as she wrote her letter. At first, she felt hesitant to begin writing, because she knew doing so would open her up to pain again. But as she made the commitment to proceed and memories surfaced—memories of her brother, their relationship, and his death—she realized that the unanswered questions about his death had impeded her recovery from grief. It is common for people who were not present at a loved one's accidental death to obsess over possible scenarios. I often suggest that clients work with active-imagination exercises, such as exercise 2-1, "Internal Communication with the Dying," in chapter 2, in order to participate in the passing and say good-bye.

As Marianne explored what could have happened the day her brother was killed, she opened to her pain, her grief began to flow, and her heart itself opened. Only then was she able to experience her deep love for James. She realized how much she still felt his presence in her life—"in energy, awareness, intensity." And at this point in the letter, Marianne felt a shift occurring: The release of her painful memories made room for a new relationship with James. Instead of obsessing on her loss, she now saw the positive changes that had occurred because of his death—for example, the family had become closer and more open with one another.

Marianne's connection with James, which she had been unable to feel at the beginning of the letter, was so strong at the end of the letter that she actually found it difficult to stop writing. She knew she could now bear the pain, experience it, and let it go. She also found that she could have a new relationship with her brother, one that was full of love and appreciation. In writing this letter, Marianne felt, she had released both James and herself.

Henri Nouwen wrote about his mother in *In Memoriam*: "In these weeks of mourning she died in me more and more every day, making it impossible for me to cling to her as my mother. Yet by letting her go I did not lose her. Rather, I found that she is closer to me than ever" (Nouwen, p. 60).

Amy's Letter

Workshop participant Amy wrote to her father, who had died eight years before. After starting her letter several times, she realized that she was avoiding the more difficult aspects of the relationship. Once she brought her resentments and regrets out into the open, the letter began to flow.

> Dear Dad,
>
> So much has happened in my life since you died. (And how often, for the first year or so, I had the thought, "Gee, I'll have to call Dad and tell him!") Although you might not understand some of what I'm up to these days, I'm sure you would be pleased to know how much I've grown, and that I'm finally on a path of my own choosing and for which I have great enthusiasm.
>
> But first let me talk a little about when you died. I am really grateful to have spent those last few months with you. We got to know one another in ways we never had before. I felt as if you

were actually proud of me, that you finally were able to see me at work. You saw me as responsible, competent, and as smart as you always thought I was! I was able to see you much mellower than you'd been when I was growing up. You were gentler, more loving, more accepting, easier to be with. And I really enjoyed being with you, the times we had the chance. I loved finding out how much we actually agreed on, after all those years of fighting one another. It made me feel good to see how pleased you were about me and how I "turned out."

I've started parts of this letter several times. I realize that I am hesitant to recount everything. However, I want to say what's so for me right now and I want to be as honest with you as I am with other people—honest without blame or guilt. So much has passed between us, so much anger, hurt, and confusion. What I feel right now is forgiveness—for you and for myself. From that place there's nothing to do except just be with you and realize how much I love you and you love me.

As much as I adore my Mommy and feel connected to her, I am realizing that *you* have had more influence on me than any-one . . . much more than I ever realized until just now. Whether I was rebelling or trying to win your approval (which seemed impossible to me as a child), whether I was emulating you and learning the many useful things you taught me, or rejecting you as a model, or trying to hurt you or whatever . . . you were the seed around which Amy formed. I think that, since you went away, I've unraveled the layers and have finally found the essence of me. It's almost as if I can re-create myself now in my relationship with you, rather than bounce off you in reaction.

I think it's probably very simple: You always loved me and didn't even think to tell me or reassure me of that—it's where you came from.

Do I have some regrets? Yes. I regret the things I did to hurt you. I regret I didn't kiss you good-bye that last night. I was afraid I'd wake you up and you'd have another seizure, but I wish I'd done it. And I wish I'd come to see your body after you had died. I don't know why . . . it was one of those things I thought about doing and talked myself out of. I try not to talk myself out of things that I feel like doing anymore.

Do I have some resentments? Yes. I resent that, because of whatever pressures you were experiencing and maybe because you didn't get much unconditional love as a kid, you were really hard on me. You always reminded me of my potential by letting me know that I wasn't fulfilling it; you often disapproved of me; you called me a "mixed-up little girl" when what I really needed was some understanding; you hit me way too much; you were rough with me when I needed tenderness; you had no respect for my feelings; you criticized me; you tried to scare me about sex rather than educate me, and you left me terribly vulnerable to the very things you were hoping to protect me from; you never told me I was pretty. It took me a long time to work through feelings of shame and to find my own self-esteem again, Dad. But I have and I will not spend the rest of my life blaming you or myself. I'm hesitant to say that I forgive you, because it sounds so ungrateful for all you did for me. I finally realized they're not connected. You did what you did for me, and you did some things that really hurt me and which I took very personally and seriously. I thank you for what you did do for me and I forgive you for what you did that wasn't loving. I forgive myself, too, and hope that you forgive me as well.

Now that the hard and ugly stuff is out in the open, maybe I could just say what I love about you and what I wish, OK? You were very handsome, Daddy, and you had a great body for a long time!

So many people loved you. You worked hard and made sure we had plenty to eat and clothes to wear. I know you loved us and you loved Mommy, and you expressed it the best you could. You took care of your brother, and your mother, and even people who worked for you. You probably did many things for people that you never told anyone about. In many ways, you were a very generous man. I wish I'd been enough of my own person to have talked with you more as a friend. Would you have talked more about personal things? Would you have shared what happened in the war or would you have always kept that to yourself, like Grandma still does? Is there anything you ever wanted to tell me that you didn't say? Would you tell me now?

Did you know that when you died they put the flag at half-mast on the common? That was incredible. You did so much for that little town. You built your business from nothing to something great and you left Mom financially secure. Thank you for all those things, Dad.

I want to ask you something. Sometimes I remember what it felt like to be a very little girl, and at those times what I want is to be held by Daddy, to be told that I'm beautiful and wonderful just the way I am and to hear you tell me you love me. Would it be OK if we did that once in a while? You don't have to say anything, just hold me and I'll know. And you'll know that I love you too, OK? Thanks, Daddy. I love you. And I miss you.

Amy had begun her letter by updating her father on her life. She then recalled her final months with him and expressed her appreciation for the time they had together. At this point, Amy admitted that she had other feelings toward her father as well, ones that were harder to express. She made a commitment to be honest with her father, without blaming him. Through the powerful statement "You were the seed around which Amy formed," Amy acknowledged that her father had had a greater influence on her than anyone else and that, as a result, his criticisms and his withholding of expressions of love had had a devastating impact on her self-esteem. Once Amy communicated her regrets and resentments, she felt ready to forgive both her father and herself. Only then could she acknowledge all the positive ways he had impacted her life, the family, and their community. By the end of the letter, Amy felt so close to her father that she asked him to hold her as her Daddy from time to time. So many adults who have lost a parent have said to me, "I just want my Mommy! I just want my Daddy!"

Charlotte's Letter

The death of Charlotte's first friend had a deep impact on her life: She was eighteen years old when he died, and she vowed never to love again. Feeling guilty that her life would go on after her friend's had ended, she put aside her dreams for her future. By the time she wrote this letter, she had emerged from "thirteen years of darkness" and was able to express both how devastating her loss had been and how much the friendship had meant to her.

Dear Donnie,

Did I ever tell you about Howdy Doody? My family was living in Texas; I think I was about seven years old. As you know, my mother, like her mother before her, would not allow me to play with other children. Consequently I was a lonely child. Howdy Doody was my friend. Then one day my mother shattered this love by telling me that he was not a real boy; he was a puppet who moved with strings attached to a stick that a man was controlling behind a curtain. My only friend wasn't real. I was crushed.

We met a few months later. They tell me that you gave me flowers from the garden. I cannot remember that incident but I can remember the joy of being with you. My very own friend! You liked me and thought that I was lovable. It was the first time that I could be in a masculine presence without fear of being hit. My skinny legs were bare from under my little girl's skirt. There was no shame. I was free to be with you. I can remember the smile that started from you to my depths, my soul, then to my heart, and then back to you again. Did you feel the same way? Were the flowers a deep red, and was the color of the stems and leaves a deep dark green?

We were eighteen when you died, and I vowed never to love again. The great effect this vow would have on my life I could not have known. The pain of losing you was so immense. The guilt of getting over this pain was equally unbearable. There was no help for me, besides, I was probably too weak and emotionally undeveloped to receive it. My solution was to shut down. No more loving and risks, no more guilt, and no more grief. I call that period my thirteen years of darkness.

Were you there when I had the vision? I saw you sitting with your one leg propped up beneath your chin, just as you used to. Then I revisited the cancer's pain and for the first time felt a huge fear. Were you as terrified of this pain as I was? I became nauseous. You looked so terrible, your growing adolescent body had withered into something grotesque. But how could I respond to this while caring for you? It took that long for me to feel the pain, the fear, and the devastation that death did to you. It has taken much longer to know how that devastation affected my life.

The next part of the vision was numinous. Your body metamorphosed into otherworldly colors of bright green and yellow. It slowly became an embryo. So beautiful! This vision was a wonderful gift. From then on, I knew that there was an afterlife.

Last May, I was cleaning house and listening to Joan Baez and Leonard Cohen. One of my favorite songs speaks of seeing one's true love. When I heard the last line, "and death had put an end to his growing," I was standing near a big chair. Suddenly, I leaned down on the chair, my heart pierced with grief of losing you. From within these words came, "I did not even know." You were my first love, and until then, I had not known. My parents never allowed me to know what was important to me. Recently I have begun to know who I am and what I feel and need. These "knowings" have reminded me of my grief and how much I still miss you.

I'm in school now. A few weeks ago, I had a dream about you. I was telling you that I was going to get a Ph.D. Then I felt such tremendous guilt. Remember that last summer, when we all spent a day at a little lake? Sharon, you, and I were sitting and talking. Sharon had just shared her dreams for the future. There I was, with kids my own age. I expressed my desire to finish college. You said, "I just want to live," and then you swam away from us. It felt so bad. Have you forgiven me? How could I be so insensitive? My guilt banished me from the hopes of making something of myself. How could I ask for the prestige of an education when you had been denied life? Now, after all these years, I am getting a Ph.D. I guess it is time to forgive myself.

You were my hope for the future. You were my first friend. If it had not been for you I do not think I could have found my husband. I still miss you and there are times when I am still angry that you are gone. Now you have begun to help me in my dreams. For this, I am grateful.

Writing this poignant letter helped Charlotte, after years of agonized grieving, build a new relationship with Donnie. Instead of feeling guilty for making something of herself, Charlotte could now proudly share her academic accomplishments with Donnie and accept his help in her dreams.

Writing a Response

The person you write to will never read your letter, of course, and can never actually respond in kind. But the techniques of internal communication allows you to frame a response to your heartfelt correspondence by engaging your imagination and opening yourself to realities that have been suppressed.

Let's look at an example of both a letter to a loved one and the response that emerged in the writer's imagination. Like many women, Ray had had a distant relationship with her father. As a young girl, she had yearned for his approval and encouragement—in fact, for any outward expression of love. Later, as she sat hour after hour with her dying father in the hospital, she treasured their moments of intimacy. She stroked her father's head and held his hand; they cried and talked together. After his death, she grieved not only the loss of her father but also the loss of new opportunities for intimacy. More than a year after his death, Ray wrote about her sadness and disappointment in a compelling letter to her father:

Driving through the green hills to the hospital, I push back tears, telling myself it will be easier to meet death in the springtime, the natural world around me singing a glorious cantata to life. I tell myself, springtime will be enough to hold me while you go on, swept along in the Great Dance. "The sheep have begun lambing," I say, trying to bring some joy to your bedside. You clasp my hand tightly, your face more candid than I have ever seen it, and softly we let the tears flow, crying together for all the lambs you'll never see in the windy fields, all the springtimes that will come and go without you.

When I think of reaching out to you now, Daddy, my heart aches. My whole being becomes aching sadness. This room where I sit in California, half a world away from any place you ever knew, feels strangely empty. I close my eyes and see you, frail, vulnerable, stripped of your stern pride. Daddy, if only you could have been soft with me before death was staring you down. If only we could have cried together now and then about the simple sad things that happen in life.

Now that there is absolutely nothing left to protect or hide, could we talk? Now that there is nothing you could possibly lose, could we be close and real? Daddy, even now I am waiting, as I always waited, for you to give me something of yourself.

I remember how at breakfast (Mummy long gone into her busy day), you'd sit across the table from me, staring over my head out the window, eating in silence. Daddy, why didn't you ever talk to me? Why was I so invisible, so irrelevant, so disappointing to you?

Did we get entangled in some mutual knot? I can't remember. Mostly I only remember the pain. And the time I saw you cry when Bess died in the bog at the edge of the pond. I know you loved that pony. But when I called from college: "Please, please bring her in this winter, Daddy. She is getting too old to winter outside." "Nonsense," you said. "She's fine." Why was it so hard for you to admit that animals, children, people need love?

In this letter, Ray has asked two crucial questions that I often read several times to workshop participants before they begin writing their dialogues: "*Now that there is absolutely nothing left to protect or hide, could we talk? Now that there is nothing you could possibly lose, could we be close and real?*" When we remind ourselves that the relationship has changed and that old protections are no longer needed, then we can take advantage of the opportunity to break out of old patterns of relating.

The dialogue did in fact provide an opportunity for Ray and her father to communicate from their hearts about painful issues in their relationship. In writing her father's response, Ray saw into her father's reasons for being neglectful and hurtful in their relationship as she had never seen before. In answer to her question, "Why was it so hard for you to admit that . . . people need love?" her father's response yielded these poignant words:

"*Because*," she wrote in his voice, "*then I'd have had to admit that I needed love. And what if I wasn't loved? What if no one loved me? That would have been too hard to bear.*"

Ray immediately reacted with a question, and quite naturally an active dialogue developed between them:

Ray: Is that why you would say those cruel things to me whenever we were alone together in the car? "Nobody likes you," you'd say. Why did you say such hurtful things?

Dad: Because you were not the child I wanted. You were too wild, too emotional, naked to the world. I couldn't show you off. You had no polished front. You were too raw, too vulnerable. You made me hate you.

Ray: How?

Dad: You weren't happy enough.

Ray: Yes, I remember when I was about seven you chiding me, "What's the matter with you? Why don't you glow like other kids?" I would sit hours in my room, studying my face in the mirror wondering why I didn't glow. Daddy, how could I glow for you? I didn't know how. Couldn't you see the light inside couldn't shine through the drowning sadness, the shame of never being enough, the ache for something I couldn't name? It was all I could do to walk the fine line, to dodge the blows, to be invisible enough to grow and leave home. Daddy, sometimes I wonder, can you see me now, prying off this awful legacy, becoming the person I never dared to dream I could be?

Rereading her father's response several months later, it became even clearer to Ray that her father had rejected her because he couldn't tolerate his *own* emotional neediness. Throughout his life he had tried to pretend that normal people don't need love; in spite of this, he became vulnerable, emotional, and raw as he was dying. Ray described him in this state as "beautiful, sadly awkward, and tragically like the child he had found so hard to love." Ray's correspondence with her father was a breakthrough in her relationship with him. Asking her father hard and painful questions, she elicited thoughtful, honest responses from him. By the end of this first dialogue, she was developing compassion and understanding for her father. Her final question, "Daddy, sometimes I wonder, can you see me now, prying off this awful legacy, becoming the person I never dared to dream I could be?" created closure to this first dialogue but opened up new topics for the next one. It seems that she now felt ready for her father to get to know the woman she had become.

To write your own response, first make sure you have truly stated your concerns in your own letter. Then, on a separate paper and in a separate sanctuary session, compose a response in the "voice" of the "recipient." This can take the form of a short reply, a letter, or a dialogue, a technique covered in the next chapter. If you write a letter, address it to yourself and start writing without judging or editing. To free the imagination and foster empathy, you can close your eyes and picture the person's face while saying your own name silently or out loud as the person would say it. You can also focus on a favored phrase or look closely at a photograph of the person. All of these may help make the person feel more accessible to you as you begin to write. After a few paragraphs you may find, as others have, that the words flow and the letter expresses more of your family member's thoughts and feelings than your own. The imagination's capacity to put you simultaneously inside yourself and inside others may feel disconcerting and unnerving but also liberating. When you have finished this letter, reread it, opening yourself to its contents.

5

Dialogues: Going Where They Take You

Dialogue is the heartbeat of human experience.
Louise Kaplan

Writing a dialogue with your loved one can take you deeper and into more unexpected, unknown places once you've opened communication with a letter, or letters, and response. This technique is especially effective when the initial correspondence has turned up particular issues you want to explore.

Initiate your dialogue by identifying the issue or concern as sensitively as you can and then expressing your feelings about it—all this on paper following your name. Then write the other person's name and open your imagination to his or her responsive words. If there is no reaction, you can ask questions to help the dialogue begin. Let the dialogue unfold spontaneously; don't interfere or control it. Be open to the unexpected and to new information and ways of relating.

Look to the things that your loved one passed on to you or to activities that you shared together to invoke the presence of the other person. For example, Caron feels her grandmother's presence every time she bakes pies, since her grandmother had taught her to bake as a child. And when I attended my niece's ordination as a deacon in the Episcopal Church, I was reciting the Nicene Creed with the rest of the congregation when I clearly heard my father's voice beside me. In the same steady, reassuring manner he had when we had attended church together throughout my childhood, he was saying the creed along with me. Feeling such a sense of your loved one's presence will help you open to explore dialogue, whether aloud or silently.

Sophie's Dialogue

As is usually the case with internal communication, the amount of time that has passed since the death has little impact on the effectiveness of the method. Almost ten years after her father's death, Sophie wrote a dialogue between herself and her father, William. In the last years of his life, a series of mini strokes had severely restricted William's movement and impaired his vision. Her mother, Karen, had devotedly nursed him for three years in their apartment, but eventually she collapsed with exhaustion. Sophie then convinced her mother to put William in a nursing home, where he died ten days later. The night before his death, Sophie visited William, and even though he seemed comatose, she spoke to him. In an emotional breakthrough, she told him, "I love you." When a nurse called Sophie the next day with the news of his death, she felt numb yet relieved that William was no longer suffering. After arranging for the cremation, she stoically went on with her life.

It wasn't until years later that she realized how much she still held him in her heart and mind, quoting him to friends and treasuring the books he had loved. In her living room stands a cherry bookcase with leaded glass doors that holds his favorite books. Sometimes Sophie imagines that her father's spirit lives behind the tattered books in that bookcase. She writes, "Today his spirit is more alive for me than in those last months of life. So it is with fear and hope that I try to engage in a conversation with Dad." Looking at an old photo of William, she began her dialogue with a question. Immediately she received a response, and from that point on, the dialogue seemed almost to write itself.

Sophie: Dad, are you here with me? I have an old photo taken after my graduation. Your handsome face is beaming and you are standing so tall.

Dad: Little Doe, baby Doe.

Sophie: You *are* here! I have sensed it. I have felt your presence lately. Can we talk, I mean *really* talk? Sometimes I feel that you hide behind your wit. I miss your wit but I prefer that we talk honestly. Just talk and be yourself with me. I want you to know that I love you.

Dad: I do love you. I guess I never said it in just so many words. Words, what hollow, inarticulate struggle this mess of verbiage!

Sophie: Can we go back nine-plus years when you were living out your last days?

Dad: Why? I was on the rack; a time of torture. You rarely visited me. "How sharper than a serpent's tooth is an ungrateful child" [a quote from *King Lear*].

Sophie: Yes, I was afraid and overwhelmed. I felt helpless.

Dad: Well, it's water under the bridge. I have been released from that body, released from that vale of tears and suffering. . . .

Sophie: We can't change the past. I guess I need to focus on my life now. But I wish that you and I could connect on a regular basis. Can we continue this dialogue?

Dad: Sure, I have all the time in the world. But you! Get on the stick, kid!

Sophie: I need to ask you, Is there anything you feel like saying to me that you were not able to say when you were alive?

Dad: Baby Doe, I do love you. I loved you then, I love you now. In spite of the bad times and the drinking—I wish I could have been more direct and said it then and showed it then.

Sophie: Did *I* ever share my feelings with you? We both seemed to hide behind our wit. I don't want to hide anymore. I simply say to you that I love you and I miss you and I feel that you live on in my memory. I want to take time out to acknowledge these feelings. Starting right now. . . .

Dad: Just don't be obsessed. Next thing, you'll be doing automatic writing and holding seances—hokum! Remember me, but live your life! Seek out joy, not tragedy. Hold the phone; let's connect again—later.

Sophie: Dear old Dad! Thank you for your gifts. Until we connect again. . . .

In this dialogue, the father's unique style of communicating comes through very clearly. Sophie hadn't expected this, nor had she anticipated that the dialogue would flow so easily. She was delighted that she had finally broken through to such a deep and honest level of interaction with her father. She had expressed her love to him, and his direct expression of love moved her profoundly.

The healing that Sophie experienced in writing this piece radiated out to her relationship with her mother too. Her mother, Karen, called Sophie soon afterward, asking her for some time to talk about dying, a subject that Karen had been avoiding. This development surprised and delighted Sophie, but it was really part of the larger process. As we will discuss in part three, bringing the light of imagination to bear on a suppressed family issue in a dialogue with a deceased person often clears away barriers in communication with living family members.

Ellen's Breakthrough

I met Ellen at a book signing; her question was one of the last of the evening: "I'm moved by the stories I've heard here tonight. But unlike my experience, these people wanted a relationship with the person who had died. What if you hated your parent? I hated my father so much that I was relieved when he died. I don't want a relationship with him." I acknowledged her feeling and confirmed that not everyone may want to do this work. I added that it is not uncommon for people to discover significant changes in the relationship with the deceased as it unfolds in the imagination and in dreams. How will we know if that relationship has changed if we don't take the time to explore the inner relationship? Ellen, clearly resistant to the idea, shook her head and sat down.

I was surprised when Ellen showed up at an "After Loss" workshop the next day. As the participants introduced themselves, Ellen made it clear that she was not going to focus on either of her parents. Her father had died of a heart attack twenty-nine years ago, and her mother had died within the last few years. Of the two, she was most angry at her father, who she couldn't imagine could be anything but hard, distant, and unloving with her. She thought that he would still ignore her as he had done throughout her childhood, sharing with us a heartbreaking memory from her childhood that exemplified how he treated her. She was eight or nine years old, playing with her friends in the street, when she noticed that her father was walking by on the sidewalk. He strode past without even a nod or a hello. He just ignored her as though she didn't exist.

Ellen informed us that she planned to use the techniques to explore some current issues with two living relatives. Toward the end of the afternoon, the participants gathered in a circle to share the results of the dialogue exercise. Ellen was the first to speak. As I looked at the pile of papers in her lap, her eyes burning with excitement, the edges of her mouth trembling with emotion, it was clear that something profound had happened. She told us that as she had heard other people's experiences in the letter-writing exercise, she had decided to take the plunge and write a dialogue with her father. She was shocked at what had transpired.

Ellen had known through others that her father had been devastated by the war—his mother had been taken to Auschwitz, his property was confiscated, and he had been interred at Dachau. He had fled the camp and his homeland and started a new life in the United States. He was tired and confused, struggling with a broken heart and a shattered identity. But Ellen had never known how these tragedies had affected their relationship. She had never known that he had been intimidated by her "harsh tongue." He couldn't bear any more pain, and so he ignored her. He asked her forgiveness.

As she probed further, asking her father questions, she discovered that underneath all that self-protection, her father loved her and was proud that she had taken happiness for herself, something he could not do for himself. After years of anger and resentment, Ellen was astounded at how much had healed in the time it took to write that dialogue. She was filled with a tender new love for the man in the silver-framed photograph in the workshop room. He was now a living presence within her, not just a memory, and she could allow him and their relationship to grow and change.

Stephanie's Dialogue with Her Grandmother

On her deceased grandmother's birthday, Stephanie wrote a dialogue with her, the grandparent to whom she felt closest. When her grandmother told her in her last years that she had lived a long life and was ready to die, Stephanie joked that her grandmother had to see her married first. Her grandmother died just a few months after Stephanie was engaged. Stephanie later moved into her grandmother's house and was still living there four years after her grandmother's death when she wrote this dialogue:

> *Stephanie*: Gramma, there's something I've always wondered about—were you happy with your life? Growing up, it always seemed so normal to me.
>
> *Gramma*: It was the simple things in life that gave me the greatest joy—the flowers in the garden. A clean house. I enjoyed the daily routine of my life.
>
> *Stephanie*: But didn't you want more?
>
> *Gramma*: By the time you knew me, Steph, I was past middle age. Don't forget that in my younger days I had worked and taught in a one-room schoolhouse. I had done some traveling. I had

married and raised two children and had already lost my husband. I had also seen many changes in the name of progress in the world. So, yes, at one point I wanted more, but then there came a time to realize what I had and to commit to that. I have been very lucky to have been close to my brothers and sisters and to have had a son and daughter and then grandchildren. This was my life. Steph, I wish the same for you. I worry about you sometimes. Don't let the wild spirit in you blind you to the simple joys around you. Life is already here; don't run away from it. Listen to it and live it.

Stephanie: I miss you, Gramma. I miss your stories. You were the connection to my past and my history. I'm sorry I didn't listen more carefully or write it all down.

Gramma: We all have those regrets. What you need is in your heart. You know the basics. I probably had too many stories! Do you have a sense of your family tree, something that connects you back in time? That's what's important. Remember that you and your sisters, brother, and cousins are the living foliage—the leaves of the tree today. One day you too will fall to the earth to make room for the next generation. In the meantime, take the life that has flowed through this tree to you and make it your own. I am proud of you already and know that if you remain connected, good things will come.

Stephanie: Gramma, I feel like I'm not really able to say anything. This is not what I expected to happen, though I really didn't know *what* to expect.

Gramma: Like you, I never got the chance to say good-bye to you either. These are a few things I would have liked to have said, but probably you weren't ready to hear them.

Stephanie: Does this mean you're leaving me? Maybe I shouldn't have done this. You had a message for me all along. You are much stronger than I gave you credit for.

Gramma: Steph, I am not the same, obviously, as you remember me. What I said to you is important. I needed to tell you those things. We have a connection, you and I, which can't be broken, but, yes, my purpose is finished here. I have been waiting and knew you would come back to hear it.

Stephanie: [*I no longer sense her presence in the house as I have since I've lived there. She is gone.*] Gramma, don't go! [*I start crying.*]

At first, Stephanie felt panic at no longer sensing her grandmother's presence; she had not intended to break the connection. Furthermore, the dialogue had yielded up very different answers than Stephanie had expected. However, Stephanie felt comforted that her grandmother, having delivered her message, was finally free to move on. In letting go of Gramma, Stephanie felt her own freedom, a freedom that was both exciting and frightening. She realized that it was now up to her to live her life fully, tapping the life force flowing through the family tree that Gramma had described.

Other Choices: Spoken and Silent Dialogues

Whatever feels most natural to you will be the most effective in producing a dialogue. For example, look at a picture of your loved one or simply close your eyes. Some people feel more comfortable talking out loud or silently to themselves rather than writing a dialogue. As with writing, just start talking, as honestly as you can. Don't edit what you are saying—just speak your truth about the relationship. It's important that you pause every once in a while and listen; you may "hear" a response internally.

Marina, an eighty-two-year-old woman, wrote to me after hearing a radio interview in which I spoke about using the imagination to gain access to the living parent within. She wanted to share with me the dramatic breakthrough she had made through talking to her father in her imagination. She would begin her process by closing her eyes and silently talking. It would not be long before she was hearing her father's response. In this way, through a series of dialogues, she began to grieve and heal from the loss of her father; he had moved away when she was a young girl and died years later without permitting her the chance for reconciliation. His absence had profoundly affected her life, for she had been left alone with a mother who was bitter and strict. Over the years after her father's death, Marina became a quiet, passive child, eventually growing into a hesitant and fearful adult.

When Marina began to talk silently with her father, she was shocked to find him so accessible after such a long separation. With each new dialogue, she felt closer to him. After a few weeks, she sensed a dramatic shift within her consciousness. No longer afraid of life, she was confident and inspired to take risks and to connect with other people. Now she initiated a number of creative projects—writing stories was one. In a relatively short time, Marina discovered how much of her life force and creativity had been locked inside her unresolved grief. As her experience dramatically demonstrates, it's never too late to heal a relationship with a deceased loved one—and never too late to awaken more fully to life.

At first, Kira did not feel ready to converse alone with her father. She felt frightened that he would hit her, as he often had when he was alive. Her first dialogue with her father took place in a therapy session. As her therapist helped move the dialogue along by asking questions and giving support, Kira talked aloud to her father and then gave her father's responses. When Kira told her father, "I hate what you did to me," her therapist interjected, "Can you tell him what he did?"

Kira: I hate that you were never there for me. I hate how inaccessible you were. I hate how the only contact I ever had with you was violence and fear. I hate how I had to just go inside myself because I was so scared of you. I'm glad you're dead. I'm glad you can't hit me anymore. I keep thinking I don't have to be scared of you anymore, but I'm still scared.

Kira then spoke her father's words, "I don't want you to be scared of me anymore." As the dialogue proceeded, Kira at times felt overwhelmed by the intensity of her anger and by her father's uncharacteristic responses. At one point, she turned to her therapist and said, "I feel really lost now. I don't know where to go." He helped her explore what she was feeling toward her father and encouraged her to speak up about everything that was bothering her. By the end of the first dialogue, Kira had stayed with her anger long enough for things to shift with her father. Throughout the dialogue, he had listened diligently to her and responded honestly and respectfully. It was clear to Kira that her father was no longer the man she had known as a child. Wanting to know him better, she stated to her therapist, "I think we're going to be friends." A week later, she felt ready to dialogue with her father alone. She spoke out loud, recording her conversation on tape. Later she transcribed what had transpired:

Kira: Papa, I'd like to talk to you. Will you come sit with me? Come sit on this side of the bed. Hi. [*He's sitting against the wall with his legs stretched out on the bed next to me.*] I miss you so much. [*Crying*] I think of you so much, Papa. It's so weird...you're right here, aren't you? Will you talk to me? I want to hear you. I want to be with you. Talk to me.

Dad: I just want to listen now.

Kira: I have some things to tell you that I could never say before. I feel so sad about how angry I've been all this time, because I'm learning how to get beneath the anger, and I feel so sad that I could never do that with you.

Dad: But you're doing it now.

Kira: Yeah . . . I want you to hear this so much. I want you to hear how much I love you. [*Crying*] I was so angry all those years, and all I could tell you was how angry I was. And what I really wanted to say was that I longed to be close to you. When I was a little girl I wanted you to hold me. I wanted you to sit with me and hold me, and stroke my hair, and tell me about the world, and help me feel safe in the world. I longed to sit in your big lap and feel your big solid hands around me, helping me feel safe. I wanted you to hug me. And it hurt so much when you pushed me away and when you scared me with your anger and your violence. [*Crying*] That's all I wanted. I didn't want to change you. I didn't want to threaten you or hurt you or compete with you or win any battles. I just wanted to be close.

Dad: Let's be close now.

Kira: Yeah, I want that with you so much. Dad, just hold me for a while.

Dad: I'm right here.

Kira: Just hold me. Just be with me. [*To myself: Let me feel this, and let it in.*] I can feel you, Dad. I can almost smell you. I can feel your big hands. Help me heal, Papa. Help me feel what hurts, so that I don't always live stuck in the pain. Just hold my hands and help me feel your presence. Are you really here? Yeah, I feel you. I want you closer. Please come closer. Yeah, that's better. Let me feel you, Papa. [*Crying*] I miss you so much.

Dad: I haven't gone anywhere.

Kira: What do you mean, you haven't gone anywhere?

Dad: I can see you right now. You look beautiful.

Kira: [*Crying*] Papa, I wanted you to say that to me so many times. I wanted you to tell me that you loved me and that you were proud of me. I wanted you to tell me that you respected me.

Dad: I was too defended.

Kira: Yeah. I longed for that person underneath all those defenses . . . the person who wrote all those love letters to Mom. I wanted to see that person.

Dad: I couldn't do it.

Kira: Why couldn't you do it? What was the wall?

Dad: I got hurt too many times.

Kira: Tell me, Pop, what hurts. Tell me what hurts for you.

Dad: I wanted to be held too. I wanted to be safe somewhere. It was never safe for me. I didn't know about that. [*Crying*] I didn't know it was possible to create that for someone.

Kira: Pop, let me hold *you*. I'll stroke *your* hair. And you can cry for a little while. I want to give that to you. I want to give it back to you. Mom taught that to me. She taught me how to feel safe. So I can give that to you now. Yeah . . . it's OK to cry. It's OK to let all that pain out. I'm right here with you. Put your arms around me. Thanks. You're with me too . . . I can feel it. I love you, Papa. I love you so much. I just want to rest here with you for a little while. I love you, Papa. I hope I can always feel you like this.

Dad: I'll always be with you when you need me.

Kira: It's so funny how much I miss you and how much I feel you here at the same time. I'm going to say good-bye now. We'll talk again soon. I love you.

Using internal communication techniques, you can talk out loud or silently to those who have died, thereby connecting with them through your imagination. Some people feel more at ease and unconstrained when they are talking, and they would most likely find this choice more conducive to letting their dialogues flow. If you later want to review what has transpired, you can record and transcribe your dialogues.

Spontaneous Dialogues

Sometimes the opportunity for an interaction through the imagination arises unexpectedly. A friend of mine was jolted out of sleep by the words, "Good morning, Lois." Shocked, she couldn't believe what she had heard, for Lois knew without a doubt that this was her father's voice. With a sudden outbreak of goose bumps, Lois realized that the morning marked the first anniversary of her father's death. Although she never again heard his voice after this initial startling experience, Lois regularly started talking to her father, afraid that if she hesitated she would lose this priceless opportunity to connect with him. Lois let her father know how much she missed him and loved him. She updated him on the events of her life since his death and reassured him that her mother was doing well and would soon be joining him. When she finished, she was filled with a deep sense of peace.

A client shared with me another story of an unexpected but meaningful dialogue with a deceased loved one. Janet felt drawn to the site of her husband's grave on the first anniversary of his death. When she arrived at the graveside and stood silently, reflecting on her loss, a conversation with her husband arose in her imagination—much to her surprise. She spoke out loud to James and heard his responses very clearly in her mind. The two discussed their daughter Claire's upcoming marriage, which James had vehemently opposed when he was alive. Claire's father now wanted to offer his blessing.

Janet was quite shaken by this experience; nothing like this had ever happened to her before. Even though she could not rationally explain the interaction, she was convinced that it had indeed been James she'd spoken with. The next day, she sent Claire a note describing her experience at the cemetery. She enclosed a check to help cover expenses for the wedding that both she and James now fully supported. Claire was deeply moved that she had received the once unattainable approval from her father.

Just as Janet found that standing at her husband's graveside inspired a dialogue with him, so sitting on her mother's bed instigated Paige to talk with her deceased mother—as though this were the most natural thing in the world. Both her mother and aunt, her last living relatives, had died in a car accident, a loss that felt unbearable to Paige at times. As she described in her letter to me eleven months after the accident, her talks with her mother gave her so much comfort that she found room for laughter in her grief:

> In the first months after Mother's and Aunt Peggy's deaths, I traveled the mile to the house which was their home. The contents of the home would have to be dissolved . . . but more importantly, their home was my sanctuary.
>
> I sat on the side of my mother's bed and talked to her, cried to her, and asked for her help. Drifting into deep thought, I began to find some peace. I'd busy myself with all the tasks and took comfort from the "things" which she dearly loved. Reality always returned by 3:00 P.M. as my children needed their mother when they returned from school; they were working through their own grief at the loss of their grandmother and great-aunt.
>
> Through the process of giving up the home in which I grew up, letting go of the physical bond between mother and daughter, the horror of tragedy, and the sorrow of loss, I never stopped talking to my mother, whether it was in my mind when I allowed myself to drift into another world or whether sitting on the corner of the bed with my words spoken aloud.
>
> I felt my mother's presence through the past months even though I could not touch her or have her put her arms around me to tell me everything would be alright.
>
> I found my mother's wisdom guiding me through the difficult decisions. I also found my mother's essence, a love of laughter,

and an approach to life in which smiles and laughter can be found in tragedy as well as triumph. I could hear her voice and the tonality of her voice encouraging laughter in spite of my tears. Her index finger waved at me as she told me, "Sell the damn house. . . . I never liked it." We'd laugh together, and we talked in my dreams.

I found that my mother will always be my mother whether in life or the life after . . . not through memories of our lives together on earth but by opening the window of my mind to the spiritual world. I hear a phrase, which I am only hearing in part, that my mother used to say to me: "There is more to heaven and earth . . ." I guess I should have listened more carefully as a child. She's waving that finger again—through my tears now, I smile.

Activities that were once shared can suddenly yield an unexpected dialogue. Judy Ashley had curled her mother's hair every week for years and did not feel confident that the funeral man could do the job as her mother would have liked. Holding a curling iron, comb, and rollers, she approached her mother's body on the steel table at the funeral home. Her hair was "straight and stiff like an old straw broom"; Judy realized she had a big task ahead of her. She started to comb her mother's hair.

> After he [the funeral man] left, I started talking to Mom. After all, we always talked when I did her hair. I didn't see any-thing wrong with it. I told her that her hair was a mess. I told her she would die if she could see it. Then I started to laugh. . . .
>
> I worked and talked. Sometimes I worried about the funeral man catching me talking to a dead body. After a while, though, there was just me and Mom. There were moments when I was sure I heard her voice. The hours passed quickly. It was just like old times (Ashley, pp. 29–30).

These stories emphasize how important it is to set aside doubts and hesitations when the opportunity for a dialogue presents itself unexpectedly. Lois, Janet, and Paige felt grateful that they had been willing, on a moment's notice, to engage in conversations with their loved ones—these were conversations that shocked but inspired them. Judy felt that it was natural and reassuring to talk to her dead mother as she curled her hair; her only concern was the funeral man's reaction if he should discover what she was doing.

You never know when the opportunity for a dialogue will present itself—upon awakening from sleep, doing a task you once shared, standing at the graveside. Even though you may feel caught off guard or self-conscious, seize this precious opportunity for connection.

Creating a Memory Book

Ken Kramer, a teacher of religion at San Jose State University, created a book to honor his father, Roy. Bringing a notebook along with him, Ken started writing as his father was dying in the hospital. While his father slept, he wrote poems to his father, reflecting on their relationship, his appreciations, and his regrets. Shortly after Roy's death and the memorial service, Ken gathered together and photocopied these poems along with photos and posters of rifles and engines. On a green paper cover, he placed a smiling photograph of Roy. Above this, Ken typed the words "Old Antique," a term Roy's close friend used to describe his buddy.

Ken feels strongly that creating this book helped him grieve and heal. By the time he completed it and sent copies to friends and family, he felt closer to his father than he had ever felt in life. Ken had actually had a pretty distant relationship with his father; the two had shared few interests and found little to talk about. Much to Ken's delight, death opened up a new, intimate dialogue with his father, as demonstrated by the dialogue that appears toward the end of Ken's book:

S: Dad . . .

F: What Kenneth? (*The exact way he would have said it, I hear, as if he is saying it!*)

S: I love you, Dad, even much more now that you are not here. You must feel it. Do you?

F: It is easier, now.

S: Now? Where are you?

F: I don't know, but I think I can know.

S: I can envision you, Dad, still pretty much by yourself even though there are others around you, some of whom you even recognize.

F: [*Laughs*]

S: Dad, I'm collecting material for a Death Book to honor you (like the birthday books I have done for the girls). Remember the birthday books?

F: Yeah . . .

S: Is there something you would especially want me to include in it, something that you are extra-proud of?

F: [*pause*] Kenneth, ya know that old [*pause*] ya know! It's in the garage. What about that?

Prompted by this dialogue, Ken went to the garage, where he found a small scrapbook tucked inside a larger one. He had never seen this book before; it was full of news clippings of incidents of death. As a teacher of a death-and-dying course at the university, Ken realized that he had inherited his father's fascination with death. He had never imagined that this interest had been in any way connected to his father. He then resumed his dialogue.

S: Dad, this is wonderful. Your scrapbook. This is a treasure. Now I see where my notebook and journal-keeping come from.

Now I discover a side of you I never, never knew—your pre-
occupation with death news.

After writing this piece, Ken had a significant dream. He was eating
breakfast when his father walked into the room and sat down on Ken's lap.
Roy then got up, walked around to the other side of the chair, and again sat
on his son's lap. This time he looked deeply into Ken's eyes and kissed
him on the mouth. Ken was deeply moved by his father's uncharacteristic
expression of love. The dream confirmed for Ken that since Roy's death
profound changes had indeed taken place in his relationship with
his father. Weeks after his father's death, Ken told me that the dialogue
initiated through the book he created continues on in his daily life. When
he sees a photograph of his father, Ken often breaks into spontaneous
conversation with him. In the course of our visit over tea, several times
Ken spoke lovingly to his father: "You taught me that, Dad!" and "Did you
hear that, Dad?"

Put together your own Memory Book using internal communication
techniques. Write letters, poems, and dialogues to your loved one. If you
sense a response from this person, write that too. Invite other family
members to contribute. You can include photographs, old letters, as well
as quotes from the memorial service or funeral. Dedicate and title your
book; create a cover. Then photocopy it. If you want to share your book,
send copies to friends and family.

As you use your imagination to create dialogues with a deceased loved
one, you will animate and enrich your internal relationship. These dialogues encourage intimate, soul-satisfying conversations—conversations
that give voice to your own *and* another's innermost thoughts and feelings.

6

Connecting through Imagery

It is the image in the mind that links us to our lost treasures; but it is the loss that shapes the images, gathers the flowers, weaves the garland.

Colette

Writing and talking with a deceased loved one may have already brought you images of this person. In this chapter, I give you some guidance in calling into your imagination and using such images intentionally to connect with the inner presence of the person who has died. With practice you'll actually be able to see, hear, and touch your loved one. Many clients have told me, "I felt that I was *really* with him. He was so vivid that I could reach out and touch him!"

Imagery, a primal language, is perhaps our first means of perceiving the world. Although we may not be aware of it, we think in imagery all the time. When cultivated, imagery is a powerful tool for healing. I like to think of images as living presences rather than as pictures. When we immerse ourselves in imagery—as we do when we dream—the images surprise, frighten, and fascinate us. They seize our hearts, fix our attention, and even sometimes take our breath away. It is only after we awaken from a dream and look back on it that the dream images become more like pictures. The following suggestions and exercises will help you stake out an image realm in which you can immerse yourself.

Enter your sanctuary space and take some time to settle down and quiet your mind. Then close your eyes and "prime the pump" by focusing on one image—a flower, a stone, a tree, a fruit. Touch it, smell it, taste it, examine it closely. When you feel satisfied that you have activated your senses through your imagination, move on to the exercises in this chapter. Identify who it is you want to meet. It doesn't matter if this person died recently or many years ago. I will offer three meeting places to help you: in a field, at the heart of a rose, and inside a star. These scenarios will launch you into your meeting in the imagination. Later, you can experiment in creating other sites to work with.

The image of the field, rose, or star acts as a doorway that you must go through. You are entering another world that communicates to you through images. Wait quietly to see what will come, whether in sight, sound, touch, taste, or smell. Imagination will bring you new pictures as well as new sensations of the person who has died. The more details you observe, the more vivid and compelling this experience will be. In fact, you may feel shaken and unnerved by how real this world of the imagination—and the consoling presence of your loved one—seems.

In each of the three exercises, you will first explore the setting, then meet your loved one, and finally let the dialogue and interaction unfold spontaneously. You may find that the person you meet is acting different than in life. Allow this to happen, paying attention to your own resistance to any new and unfamiliar ways of relating. You may not understand the exchange that occurs while you are performing the exercise, but if you write down the dialogue, you'll have a chance to study it later. Of course, nonverbal communication or silence won't be recordable, so try to keep your memory sharp. Also, the person may want to show you something during your meeting. Be receptive to any images that appear, however absurd, disturbing, or confusing they may be. Trust that your imagination is taking you where you need to go for healing. And when you have completed this exercise, spend some time alone in your sanctuary to reflect on what has happened. In particular, notice any changes in your feelings toward the person you have met with in your imagination.

Exercise 6-1
CONNECTING THROUGH IMAGERY: THE FIELD

First you will sit down at a little distance from me—
like that—in the grass.... You will sit a little closer to me,
every day... at the same hour.... If you come at just
any time, I shall never know at what hour
my heart is ready to greet you.
Antoine de Saint-Exupery

Close your eyes. Take a few deep breaths and focus on the movement of each as it flows in and out of your body. Let the breath be your bridge as you shift your attention from the outer world to an inner world of the imagination.

You are standing in a large field that rolls out to the horizon. You see a figure approaching across this field. As the person comes nearer, you realize this is the one you hoped to meet. Be aware of what you are feeling. Notice how this person looks and moves, what he or she is wearing. Has the person changed? Be willing to let go of old pictures; your loved one may look and act in a different way than you remember. Stay in the present with this person, letting your interaction unfold without editing or interfering with what happens.

Let your loved one know how you have felt since the death—what you miss, what you regret, what you appreciate about him or her. Update the person on what has changed for you since the death and take time to listen to all responses and messages. Follow this exchange wherever it may go.

When you feel ready, tell your loved one good-bye. Watch as the person leaves, remaining aware of how you are feeling. Spend some time alone with yourself, reflecting on this experience. Then open your eyes.

Exercise 6-2
CONNECTING THROUGH IMAGERY: THE ROSE

And yet what they are looking for could be found in one single
rose.... The eyes are blind. One must look with the heart.
Antoine de Saint-Exupery

Closing your eyes, imagine a rosebud that is still tightly closed. Use all your inner senses to experience this flower: What color is it? How does it feel?

The rose is now beginning to open slowly, petal by petal. At its center stands your loved one, waiting for you. Go to meet the person and allow your interaction to unfold on its own. You may be surprised at what happens between you—some interaction or communication could take place that you never imagined possible in life.

This is a time to update your relationship. Share with this person the changes, feelings, insights, and new perspectives you have experienced since the death.

When you are ready, conclude your visit. If you still feel unfinished, let the person know when you will be visiting again. Then step out of the rose's center and watch the petals fold up again, enclosing and protecting the place of your meeting.

Exercise 6-3
CONNECTING THROUGH IMAGERY: THE STAR

In one of the stars I shall be living. In one of them I shall be laughing.
Antoine de Saint-Exupery

Close your eyes and imagine yourself sitting on a hill. Above you stretches the night sky with thousands of stars glimmering against a background of black. Thinking of a loved one who has died, let your eyes wander over the entire sky until one star begins to stand out. Looking at this star, observe the threads of light that emanate from its center. One of these threads shines down to where you sit. Follow this beam up to the star. As you move closer and closer, the intense light may blind or overwhelm you. It may take some time for your eyes to adjust.

When you reach the star, step into its center. Your loved one will be waiting for you. Take all the time you need to get reacquainted. Discuss any unfinished business between you; share resentments and regrets as well as appreciations. Then explore your relationship as it is now. Acknowledge the changes, no matter how subtle.

As you prepare to leave, you will be presented with a gift to take back with you. Receive this and descend back to earth on the thread of light.

Sue's Story

Imagery has the power to connect the living and the dead within the imagination. This connection takes place on many levels at once, making it a profoundly moving and transforming experience. You not only hear the words of the person you had thought lost to you, but you can also see and touch this person. In holding the image of this person in your mind, you create and re-create the relationship, not necessarily as it was but as it is now.

I saw my father two years after his death. I found myself in an old rose garden with climbing vines, old gnarled trees, and tangled roses. At first I embraced an oak tree until an old rose bush called to me. He was the grandfather rose of the garden, planted in dark rich soil; his trunk was twisted and knotted, his leaves covered in lemon-white flowers tinged with crimson. I bent toward the fragrance and saw one rose open. My father stepped from its center and grew to his full height.

My father wore a beige, yellow, and gray Pendleton shirt and tan khakis; he slowly took off his glasses, put them in his pocket, and took my hand. I noticed his long, tapered fingers, still artistic and yet covered with wrinkles and tanned from working in the garden. I told him how much I loved him, and we hugged each other easily, unlike years ago when it was so awkward. Then I asked my father to hold me in a rocking chair. He said he would love to, that he tried to hold me when I was a child, but I was too active and eager to jump off his lap to play outdoors.

A wooden rocking chair appeared with gold stenciling on the back like the one in our den at home. Down we sat. I could feel the soft yet rough texture of the Pendleton against my cheek, its pocket and buttons. My father smelled clean like Camay soap.

Then we walked together holding hands. I told him of my complete love, joy, and peace in his presence. We turned to each other, and as we did, the past and all its pain vanished. "Daddy, my God! We have healed the past. We have healed the past for us both. All that matters is the love I feel for you and the love you feel for me." My father asked for my forgiveness for the suffering he had caused me; he cried and hung his head. I raised his dear face in my hands and said, "All is forgiven. I know you did the very best you could, and now is all that matters."

We sat on an old tree stump in the garden, relishing each other's company, laughing and talking. Soon it was time to go, and I helped him step into the rose, and it enclosed him once more. I kissed and blessed the rose, thanking it for holding my father in its embrace. "Good-bye Daddy. I'll be back." I walked out of the garden into the trees, feeling the wind swirling around me.

Candace's Story

Candace's father died the first time for her when she was three years old. He joined the U.S. Navy and left to fight in the war. Her gentle father returned an incurable and irresponsible alcoholic. By the time he died twenty years later, Candace had already given her father up for dead. At the time, Candace was pregnant, and her obstetrician advised her not to go to the funeral, for fear that the stress would be too much. She was secretly relieved at his counsel, but years later her unresolved grief surfaced and made itself known through a debilitating physical ailment. In finally facing the loss of her father, she turned to meditation, prayer, dreams, painting, and writing activities, which often yielded rich imagery. A clear mind, empty page, and blank canvas are all fertile arenas where healing images can take form. In a class she was introduced to the rose exercise.

> The rose in my garden is withered and dead-looking, faded cream without much hue, most petals already fallen to the ground. It seems appropriate. Nevertheless I ask for it to open, and as I do, before my eyes the rose metamorphoses into a large and splendidly beautiful, healthy flower. Out steps my father, a young man in his late twenties. We sit down on my patio. I begin to vent my anger at him for abandoning me and ruining my life. I expected nothing from him this time either. But I wait to see what might happen.
>
> I find myself on the front steps of St. Patrick's Cathedral in New York. I walk to the doors, open them, and see my father, a bishop in full regalia, walking down the aisle toward me but oblivious of my presence. Back on the patio, I say to him, "I had no idea you wanted to be a priest!" He tells me that his unfulfilled dream of becoming a medical doctor was not so far afield. Medicine was the more acceptable path to pursue; he followed neither.
>
> Next I am on the shore of a large rustic lake in St. Louis. A boy, all in white and wearing knickers and a tie, is standing in a

small wooden boat. He is helping a girl, dressed in soft white filmy cotton, climb into the boat. I am straining to see if it is my mother. Again, much to my amazement, she is a lovely child with whom he is much in love, not my mother. I hear him say about my mother, "She was insufferably vain!" I recognize his frustration and empathize with his recognition. My mother had told me reams of stories of how she was wooed by this and that man and how she settled for my father. Never once did I hear about my father's past.

"But who is this girl?" I ask him. He tells me he knew her for years. She eventually married a wealthy man who would take care of her. After my dad married my mother, he saw this friend once or twice, but he stayed married to my mother, largely because of me, he said, and because divorce was absolutely unacceptable in his eyes and to his family and the Catholic Church.

I find myself in a bright and airy bedroom of a large Victorian home. I see the high ceilings, an open window facing the tree-lined street as a curtain blows gently in the breeze. I see no one, but I sense my dad is there alone. The room feels lonely. Has someone died? Yes, my grandfather has died, and his son is in the vacated death room, desperately trying to sort out a loss that is too large for this twelve-year-old boy and youngest of six to hold. I get the sense that the boy was not allowed in the room earlier to say good-bye to the dying man.

Next it is World War II, and my dad is a battleship navigator in the South Pacific. The day is spring clear, warm, and sunny. And suddenly I get this picture of a very tan and healthy looking man who says to me, "I actually liked being in the Navy. I had to admit to myself at this time that, although I missed you and your mother terribly, I also liked being away from your mother and grandmother." My mother's mother had been loving but controlling; she never was to relinquish her daughter to a man. I begin to cry, tears of compassion and understanding. I had only heard my mother's side of the stories.

I am invisible in the St. Louis kitchen; my dad in uniform, mother and grandmother are seated at the table. Daddy is saying he wants to leave. He cannot imagine how the marriage can ever work. He doesn't want to hurt anyone. My mother and grandmother are manipulating the situation; my father succumbs and agrees to stay. He returns from his leave back to the war. This comes as sheer news to me that he had ever tried to end an even-then-unworkable relationship. My parents had seemed so happy to me as a little girl.

The last thing I do in this meeting is to tell Daddy how sorry I am for the way his life turned out. I am feeling more forgiving and less accusatory. Then my father says to me, "I am so sorry!" I know he is, but for so many years I have refused that. Being sorry doesn't change anything; what it can do is get someone pretty easily off the hook. So I tell him I want to be released. I want him to do whatever he can wherever he is, over there or in a new life, to make it up to me. Release me and in so doing release himself.

As for so many people, in this encounter the images did not unfold as Candace had expected. They seemed to have a life of their own as they led her through vignettes of her father's life. Having worked with active-imagination techniques before, Candace trusted the flow of imagery and was careful not to interfere. By the end of the exercise, she felt that for the first time she had experienced her father's life through *his* eyes rather than through her mother's.

These images were both unnerving and healing for Candace. They allowed her to contact her father in a caring and compassionate way; the person she spoke to was the kind, caring, sensitive, wise, and highly intelligent man she had known as a young girl. Through the vivid vignettes, she was able to experience her father's disappointments and unlived dreams and for the first time to understand the factors that had contributed to his alcoholism.

Through the imagination you can enter another's body or life experiences, making it possible to see the world through that person's eyes. In this way, empathy develops naturally, transforming old hurts and resentments into understanding and compassion.

Meeting a Son and Meeting a Mother

Richard started therapy when stress at work began to endanger his health. After a few sessions it became clear that underlying his stress was the somber presence of a grief he felt hopeless to resolve—his son, Brian, had died of AIDS five years before. It had been devastating for Richard to watch Brian's body deteriorate and to witness his suffering helplessly. These memories haunted him by day, and grief gnawed mercilessly at his gut at night.

In one of our sessions, Richard, though doubtful, agreed to try the rose exercise. To his great surprise, a clear image of Brian manifested itself as soon as the rose opened. Brian smiled and assured Richard that he was at peace; he reported that he had felt frustrated trying to let his father know this. They proceeded to talk about their relationship, healing some old wounds that had plagued them both for years. When Richard opened his eyes, he looked immensely relieved—his face was clear and radiant, qualities that often accompany a dramatic opening of the heart. Richard told me he only regretted having waited so long to come to this place of healing. He had never dreamed this kind of breakthrough was possible by means of the imagination!

Another client, Lela, chose the field exercise, hoping to meet Anya, her mother, who had died several months earlier. Lela had not been present when Anya passed away. She had left the hospital for a dinner break, returning to find her mother gone. Ever since, she had agonized over being absent at the time of Anya's passing and had obsessed over what she could have done to keep her mother alive. Originally, Anya's decline resulted from a simple accident from which Lela had expected her mother to recover easily. However, as unforeseen complications set in, Anya's health and spirits rapidly deteriorated. Lela regretted that she had not been aggressive enough with the doctors and that she had not pushed for other medical options. Over and over in her head, Lela would replay the progression of her mother's illness, condemning herself for all the mistakes she felt she had made.

Now, as she focused on the field in her imagination, Lela saw her mother as clearly as though she were alive. As soon as Anya appeared, the images became brilliant. Lela talked with her mother for a long time about her guilt and anguish, and then she listened to what Anya had to say. Anya told her that she had wanted to die. Having concluded her commitments and knowing that her children were taken care of, she had felt ready for this step into the unknown. She had avoided telling Lela about this decision because she knew her daughter would resist.

Anya's words astounded Lela, yet she knew that her mother's perception was true. If, in real life, Anya had told her that she wanted to die, Lela would have resisted and fought, completely unready to let her mother go. Anya's revelation released Lela from her guilt, and in its place she experienced a deep love for her mother. Lela was finally able to focus on letting Anya go.

Healing consists in receiving—rather than repressing—the images that the imagination sets before us. Putting aside their assumptions and expectations, Richard and Lela embraced their loved ones—and their messages—as they appeared in the exercises. These potent images brought Richard and Lela to the edge of the known and restored the family members lost to them.

Unanswered Questions

Miriam attended an "After Loss" workshop six months after her twenty-two-year-old son had committed suicide. As do many parents in this situation, she agonized over his suicide. Feeling that she had failed as a mother for not picking up on her son's subtle signs of distress, she obsessed over what she could have done to prevent his death. There were so many unanswered questions, the biggest of which was "Why?"

In the workshop, Miriam welcomed the opportunity to write her son a letter; she poured out how much she missed and loved him, along with the thoughts and feelings that she had been experiencing in the months since his death, including her feelings of anger, guilt, and rejection. She asked the questions that had kept her awake night after night. The dialogue exercise was healing too, as many of her questions were answered, except for the big question, "Why?" Later in the afternoon, I guided the group in the rose exercise. Miriam closed her eyes and focused inwardly on a crimson rose. It was unfolding petal by petal. At its center stood her grown son, standing tall and smiling broadly. Miriam reached out to him, eager to touch him after all the painful months of grieving. As she held him close to her, she thought her heart would explode with joy—she could feel him! After some time, her son took her hand and spoke, "Let me show you what I can do now." The two of them rose into the sky and then flew together. As she watched him spreading out his arms and soaring through blue space, she realized that her son was free, lightened of the burdens that had weighed on him so heavily in life. Without words she had received her answer to the question that had plagued her since her son's death. Through working with the letter, dialogue, and guided imagery exercises she felt more at peace—with her son and with herself.

Amy's father died in a plane accident when she was seven years old. She had pleaded with her father not to go flying that day, but he had taken off anyway, with his family watching from the ground. Moments after the plane took off, it exploded. Amy had never fully grieved, having learned to accept her mother's reasoning that her father had died doing what he loved.

When her father stepped out of the rose, Amy was stunned to see him so clearly, for she had held him as a memory, not as a person. With her father standing before her—so vital, loving, and whole—she realized how much she had missed him. After fourteen years, there was so much to catch up on. She talked with him about her present life, about growing up without him. She finally was able to ask him the question that had haunted her since childhood: "Daddy, why did you leave us?" He responded that he had not wanted to leave his family. He knew that his daughters would feel abandoned by him, which caused him great distress as he was dying. However, as much as he wanted to stay, it was simply his time to die. He wanted her to know that death was not the separation that she thought it was. This brief encounter with her father in her imagination left Amy glowing. Relieved by his message, she understood that he had not wanted to leave her and knew now without a doubt that he was still within her.

The Power of Imagery: A Review

As we prepare a fertile environment for imagery to come forth, the wise imagination yields to us the very images that we need for healing. Trust these images; receive and embrace them; experience them with all your senses. The more detail you focus on, the more powerful, immediate, and compelling this experience will be. Open yourself to the shock of wonder and joy. Whenever your intellect interferes with judgments or editing, gently bring your awareness back to the flow of images. Treasure and savor the images that come to you; revel in their healing touch. Let them work on you long after the exercise is over. If you carry inside images of your loved one, they may imbue your day with the presence of the other. You may also want to treat these episodes as you would movie clips that encompass meanings to think about later.

Let's review the steps for working with internal communication through imagery:

- Identify who you wish to see, and think about the problems and unresolved issues in your relationship. How have these affected your feelings about this person since the death?
- Set aside a period of uninterrupted time in your sanctuary. Sit down, focusing your attention on your breathing. Let your mind clear and your body settle.
- Close your eyes and, in your imagination, go to a healing place (such as a garden, field, forest, special room, or beach). Explore this environment with all your senses.
- Invite the person to visit you in the place you have chosen for the purpose of healing your relationship. Watch carefully as he or she approaches. Be aware of how you are feeling. You may observe changes in the person; don't hold on to old memories.
- Begin a dialogue, addressing the issues of concern to you. Speak honestly. Don't interfere with what naturally unfolds. You can also just be with this person, sharing the time together in silence.
- Listen carefully and respectfully to the response.
- Be receptive to unexpected developments. For example, the person may take you somewhere or give you something. Someone else may appear.
- Bring your encounter to a close. If you still feel unfinished, tell your family member that you will be soon meeting again in your imagination.
- Spend some time in your sanctuary after the person has departed. Relax and reflect on what has happened.
- Write down what you have experienced. It may take time to understand the meaning or significance of what happened.

Using internal communication, we can discover that death need not cut us off from those we love. Through writing a letter or a dialogue, through talking out loud or working with imagery, we have new possibilities for healing old wounds, bringing our relationships up to date, and expressing our love. We come to realize that our relationships with deceased family members still have tremendous potential for growth. Any breakthroughs or healing we experience with those who have died can enhance our capacity to have meaningful and fulfilling relationships with those who are living.

Part Three

Reaching Outward

The only thing keeping you from deep, satisfying, soulful relationships is your imagination.

Thomas Moore

7

Family Communication after a Death

We became for each other new people with new lives and perspectives.
Henri Nouwen

The upheaval in the family system after a death can put considerable strain on communication amongst those who are grieving, as Liana discovered after her father's death:

My father died nine months ago. His death was a huge loss, much bigger than I had thought it would be. We had been very close but it wasn't until he died that I realized how much I had taken for granted his quiet support. I miss him terribly and feel so alone. There's an ache in my chest that won't go away—even when I'm with my husband and children. It's scary to feel this alone.

Now what's concerning me most is my relationship with my mother. I realized soon after my dad died that I wanted to heal this relationship, with all its years of pain and anger, because she is the only parent I have left. I remember thinking, "Oh my God, if my mom dies now, it'll be so much worse. It'll be by far the worst loss I have ever gone through because I will not have reconciled. We will never have an understanding of each other."

After my father's death there have been huge explosions between my mother and me. Suddenly I saw the dynamics of our relationship so clearly. We've danced around each other for years, without really seeing one another. And when my father died, I felt I was finally seeing my mother—and I didn't like what

I saw. I didn't respect her. I felt she was narcissistic and too insecure to stand on her own. The thought of being like her really scared me. I realized I had lost the one parent who could support me emotionally and was angry at being left with a parent who I thought didn't understand me. A few months ago, I tried to tell her what I was going through in my grief, but she couldn't hear me. She was too caught up in her own grief. I see now how I've played a game of being the good daughter with her, at the expense of being myself with her.

It's agonizing now to get together with her. I can no longer play the old roles, and so we don't know how to be with one another. We're both at a loss and we just feel lonely when we're together. I want so much to feel love for her. I want to be able to forgive her for...

Liana's voice trailed off, and her eyes, which had been fixed on me throughout her story, now gazed back down at her hands. She had caught herself just as she was about to blurt out some family secrets. This was territory she was unready to venture into as yet, and I respected that. We'd come back to this in a later session. When she looked up, I nodded. She looked relieved as she continued her story:

My brother has cut off all communication with my mother and me because he is going through a terrible time. He's working through his grief and the fact that he didn't reconcile with my father. It's hard to believe, but he took things a lot harder than I did. I know my mother is having a hard time understanding this. I'm sometimes caught in the middle, but I think I understand what he's doing, so I can respect his need to become comfortable with saying, "Sorry, but I can't deal with this right now." He's entitled to that, and it's no reason for him to feel guilty. It's not my job to take care of him. You can't shelter people from their pain. But I miss him so much. It's tragic that our family is so cut off from one another at the time we all need one another so much.

I had hoped my husband would help me out of my pain and loneliness. But we've had trouble communicating too. He tries to be supportive, but he's never lost a parent and he has no idea about what I'm going through. He seems intimidated by the intensity of my emotions. And I'm realizing now that I don't really trust him with my feelings, especially when they are so raw and vulnerable. Too many times he's been sarcastic with me. I feel so alone.

Bringing her hand to her chest, Liana broke into loud sobs. Her anguish was so excruciating that I could understand why her husband had withdrawn from her. I took a big breath. I couldn't take her pain away, nor did I want to. It was important that she experience it fully in that moment in the presence of another human being who also knew that pain. I encouraged her to let the tears come; I knew that her tears were leading her back to herself.

How Grief Changes Families

Grief affects different kinds of family systems in different ways, so I'll limit my remarks here to the family of origin. We'll focus on marriages and other partnerships in chapter 8.

With grief comes a heightened capacity to recognize with great clarity conditioning and patterns of relationship. Painful insights into issues that may have been overlooked or avoided now slip past lowered defense mechanisms, and problems become magnified. I have been impressed with the number of my clients and interviewees who have used this metaphor: "Since the death, it's as though a veil has been lifted. I'm seeing everything differently." This clear sight is an opportunity to appreciate the strengths of a relationship, to address its unhealthy aspects, and to develop more authentic ways of relating. The sense of freedom and new possibilities in the relationship can be exciting and terrifying.

This shift in perspective, plus a sense of her own aloneness, contributed to the changes Liana was experiencing in her relationships within her family. In her loneliness, she had been thrown back on herself and had been forced to evaluate relationships she had previously taken for granted. It was painful for her to see the compromises she had made in her relationship with her mother and husband as well as to face the absence of support and intimacy in both, especially at such a significant time of loss. As with many people who are grieving, Liana felt a yearning to improve and deepen her relationships. In particular, she knew that she wanted a more loving and authentic relationship with her mother, but with so much anger and resentment constantly surfacing, Liana had no idea how to begin.

As Liana's story demonstrated, a system in place over many years can be thrown into chaos and upheaval after the death of a family member. Old patterns don't work with the same results; past resentments, rivalries, and jealousies surface. Along with unresolved issues that may go back to childhood, new tensions and resentments can build up over issues of care for the dying person. Also—famously—the distribution of the estate of the deceased may become a major area of contention, fostering anger and family feuds.

Furthermore, alliances within the family shift after the death, creating new dynamics in the family pattern. For example, a client, Derrick, described the profound changes he had experienced in his relationship with his brother since his father's death. Derrick's brother and father had been very close, and Derrick had felt overpowered and overshadowed by his brother. However, when their father died, the family constellation changed. Suddenly the brother was left without an ally and therefore had less power than before. Derrick felt confident in standing up to his brother and fully expressing his own talents.

As families undergo such shifts, fighting may increase. Many feel confused by and even ashamed of this fighting. If family members can focus on the underlying issues and communicate with one another, this can be a time to create healthier relationships.

Finally, the awareness of mortality that death brings can be a powerful incentive to work on family relationships. Liana's realization that she had only one parent left motivated her to work on healing her relationship with her mother despite the pain and anger her efforts brought her. The death of one parent often breaks through our resistances and hesitancies in making necessary changes with the other. Nate told me how the death of his father had forced him to look at and change ways that he had related to his mother. The close relationship with his father had allowed him to overlook the difficulties with his mother: "My greatest fear in losing my mother is that I will spend a lot of time feeling very repentant about not treating her better. If she were to die today, I would wish that I had been more patient, less judgmental. Every day I think about this, and I think there's a way to prevent that kind of regret and remorse. I work toward it; I've made improvements in a few months."

Changes occur with siblings too. The death of a family member can bring siblings together with a new appreciation for this special family bond, and increased willingness and incentive may surface to work through unresolved issues toward more clarity and connection. Siblings may feel freer to talk about childhood rivalries, jealousies, and secrets that may have contaminated the current relationship. With so much coming to the surface, this is a powerful time to heal these grudges and establish a mature adult relationship with one another. In *In Memoriam*, Henri Nouwen writes about the transforming effect his mother's death had on his relationship with his siblings:

> This new closeness that we began to feel was something far greater than what is expressed by the remark, "You still have each

other." We became for each other new people with new lives and new perspectives. Life started to reveal itself in new ways. I was not simply saying farewell to her; I was also letting go of something in myself that had to die. I also perceived this in my father, my brothers and my sister. Old boundaries that had maintained certain distances between us were being lifted so that new intimacies could grow (Nouwen, p. 37).

Sometimes there is the opportunity to get to know a family member with whom the relationship had been more distant. A woman in one of my workshops had never spent any time alone with her father. She did not know who he was as an individual apart from his role in his marriage. Whenever her father had answered her telephone calls home, he had automatically handed the phone to her mother.

After her mother's death, my client felt awkward at first whenever she was alone with her father. As the weeks passed, though, she felt excited about getting to know him and started to enjoy spending time with him. When he died six months later of a heart attack, she felt grateful for this brief quality time together.

Still, there can be difficulties—fights, regrets, and resentments with a remaining parent or sibling. With both grieving simultaneously but in different ways, interactions can take on an intensity and rawness that had not been present before. With the new clarity of vision resulting from the crises, the adult child may be unable to ignore unhealthy patterns or issues in the relationship that had been long suppressed. Discussions, confrontations, and—it is to be hoped—breakthroughs can be the fascinating, and productive, result.

How can we effect the changes we desire in the midst of the emotional chaos that grief brings to a family? Communicating with family members and friends can be very hard during grief. Emotions are stirred up then, and people often feel raw and on edge. Those who are grieving often act in ways that would seem unthinkable at other times, expressing anger, impatience, and other "negative" emotions. They take risks and speak their minds with sometimes brutal honesty. They do not have the energy for being nice, taking care of other people's feelings, holding back, or engaging in old unproductive behavior patterns. There can be a sense of liberation for those who are grieving, as they discover that they actually feel better when they express themselves truthfully and authentically. If family members are all grieving at the same time, it is common for fights to break out, misunderstandings to take place, and even contact to be severed. Those outside the circle may be shocked and disturbed by these changes in behavior, and this can have a destructive effect on communication as well.

Withdrawal as a Tool for Change

Where fighting surfaces, temporary withdrawal from the relationship can be a powerful tool. Still, it can be hard to trust that pulling back from a living parent or sibling may eventually generate healing and the desire to reconnect. I experienced this uncertainty personally after my father died. The power of the forces of grief erupting in me then would not let me set aside my own feelings to focus on my mother's needs. I needed to pull back from my mother in order to honor and fully experience my own grief. Since childhood I had been conditioned to take care of my mother's needs before my own, and this pattern had become so woven into the fabric of our relationship that I did not even see the full extent of it until after my father's death—humbling for a therapist to admit. While this awareness and the ensuing change in my behavior created great discomfort at the time, I felt grateful for the developmental push my grief delivered to me. Not only did my mother and I connect again months later with a new appreciation for our differences, but I experienced an appreciable shift in making my needs count in my other relationships as well.

While distancing can provide a breathing space, it is important that it be a *phase* in creation of change, not a permanent stance. Author and psychotherapist Harriet Lerner advises in *The Dance of Intimacy*,

> Slowly moving toward more connectedness rather than more distance with members of our own kinship group is one of the best insurance policies for bringing a more solid sense of self to other relationships. When we have few connections with extended family, and one or more cutoffs with a nuclear family member (a sibling or parent), our other relationships may resemble a pressure cooker, particularly if we start a family of our own. The degree to which we are distant and cut off from our first family is directly related to the amount of intensity and reactivity we bring to other relationships (Lerner, p. 214).

Using Internal Communication

Although external communication at such an emotionally charged time may contribute to increased tension and fighting, the same resources that enable reconnection with the deceased can help us link to our living family members in a new and strengthened way. Imagination provides a safe place to pull back, reassess, and experience the relationship inwardly, and internal communication affords the opportunity to do the healing work.

Where communication has broken down or has been cut off by grief, imagination can build a bridge between you and a family member across a chasm of hurt, disappointment, misunderstanding, and anger. As you have seen, in your imagination you have freedom to address issues that have been silenced, to express yourself without restriction, and to give voice to repressed feelings. You can step inside another and experience the relationship through his or her eyes, since in the imagination you are not limited to one body. And you can watch *yourself* in the relationship while simultaneously participating in it.

All this you can do within yourself, without the other's participation—a remarkable opportunity when communication seems impossible in everyday life. In offering fresh resources to break through destructive patterns of relating and to create new perspectives that foster compassion and understanding, the imagination will help you deepen bonds, heal rifts, and express love in ways that you never dreamed possible in your everyday experience.

Sometimes work with the imagination within a family results in surprising changes in the other person. A client used exercise 7-1, presented later in this chapter, to talk to her living father about issues in their relationship that had driven them apart for years. Their communication had become limited to a few superficial gruff exchanges. A few days after doing this exercise, she talked to him on the phone and then reported to me, "I couldn't *believe* how he listened to me—he's never done that before. We talked about several important issues without screaming at each other. Something has opened up in our communication that I didn't think was possible."

Practice in the imagination not only lays the groundwork for an external discussion with a living family member but also seems to affect the discussion itself. After a confrontation with her sister, one of my clients told me, "After my mother died, I could no longer ignore the conflicts between my sister and me. Since she was the only member of my family left, I wanted a closer relationship with her. For weeks I confronted my sister in my imagination, using internal communication techniques my therapist had taught me. As I gained more clarity about my needs as well as compassion for her failings, I felt ready to talk to her. My discussion with my sister turned out very much like one I had had in my imagination. My sister was willing to listen to me. Usually she cuts me right off if I'm telling her anything that might be in any way critical of my father. But this time she was more receptive and understanding than any other time I can remember. Our relationship is different now. For the first time in my life, I feel at ease with my sister."

In tapping the imagination, we access a much greater knowledge than our conscious mind can grasp. Therefore, it is critical that you approach this work with humility and receptivity. As with your work with a deceased loved one, set aside any preconceived ideas of content or outcome, and avoid imposing what you want. Dare to receive whatever happens without judging or editing it. Allow yourself to be stretched. Images may occur that surprise, fascinate, and even horrify you. The imagination is naturally open and creative. It doesn't differentiate between negative and positive, between ecstatic and horrific, between life and death. It encompasses all this, moving us past the borders of our limited perspectives and offering the potential for healing beyond our wildest dreams.

Throughout this and succeeding chapters, guided exercises using internal communication will help you voice unexpressed feelings, gain new understanding and compassion, and face and reexperience negative situations that are currently affecting a relationship with a living family member. As you practice internal communication, you'll find yourself getting better at it, speaking out and listening more easily within your imagination. But the benefits will not stop there. Confronting a loved one in your imagination will give you the confidence to take more risks externally—to speak honestly, set boundaries, and ask for what you want. For this reason, after working with the internal communication techniques described here, you may want to initiate a face-to-face conversation with the family member in order to integrate new breakthroughs, understandings, and insights into your relationship. Keep the questions on pages 135–36 nearby in order to assess your readiness to talk to the person. Then define your goals, identify your topics, make the initial contact, pick a safe place, and set guidelines for a productive and healing discussion.

Reclaiming Freedoms

Family pioneer Virginia Satir describes five freedoms that are essential to healthy relationships in a family:

1. The freedom to see and hear
2. The freedom to say what one thinks and feels
3. The freedom to feel what one feels
4. The freedom to ask for what one wants
5. The freedom to take risks for oneself

In creating healthy family relationships, a person needs to reclaim these specific freedoms.

The following exercise will help you regain these freedoms—or claim them within your living relationship for the first time—through internal communication. Start by setting aside an uninterrupted period of time in your sanctuary. Review the questions below, which are designed to focus your attention on the work at hand. Then, perhaps using a picture of the family member you will be focusing on in this exercise, follow the procedure closely.

Assessing Family Relationships

· What qualities are now important to me in my relationship?
· What am I unwilling to put up with anymore?
· Am I satisfied with the quality of my relationships?
· What changes have occurred in my relationship with family members? What do I want in my relationships with them?
· As roles and responsibilities change as a result of the death, have any resentments or appreciations remained unexpressed?
· Has the living relationship been affected by the death?
· In going through this period of stress and grief, what strengths and weaknesses have emerged in the living relationship?
· What patterns in my parents' marriage do I see reflected in this relationship with a living family member?
· How have my friendships changed? Which friendships have grown closer? Which have grown apart?

- Am I willing to let my family and friends know what I want in my relationships? Am I able to express to them what I think and feel?
- Am I successful in becoming closer to my family and friends? In setting boundaries with them?
- How authentic am I able to be? How much have I compromised myself? Am I able to take risks in my relationships to attain what I want?

Once you reflect on these questions and clarify your priorities, you can take steps to align your relationships with your deepest longings. But there's a cautionary note: As you begin to act, be prepared for considerable disruption and conflict in your relationships.

Exercise 7-1
AN INTERNAL ENCOUNTER WITH A LIVING FAMILY MEMBER

To perform this exercise, sit down, close your eyes, and bring your awareness to your breathing for a few minutes to settle your body and mind. Now imagine a healing place. This can be a place you have seen or visited in ordinary reality, or it may be a place that exists solely in your imagination. Perhaps it exists in nature—a forest, beach, waterfall, mountaintop, garden—or is a special room. You may decide on one particular place only to find that another image presents itself instead. Don't fight this; trust what happens spontaneously.

Experience this place with all your senses. Look around and pay attention to details. Touch, smell, listen. Activating your inner senses is a critical step in this exercise. The more fully attuned you are in your imagination to all your senses, the more intense this experience will be. Continue to explore this environment with your senses until you feel fully present in your body in this place.

When you feel ready, invite the chosen person from your family to join you in this healing environment. As this individual approaches, focus your awareness on any physical sensations you are experiencing. Rather than anticipating what may happen, pay close attention to the person's expression, movements, and dress. Be aware of what you are feeling.

Some people, feeling too anxious to talk with the family member alone even in the imagination, ask for a guide to support and protect them. Standing beside you or behind you, this guide may not actively participate in this encounter but may help you simply by being present.

Begin to address the issues that are of concern to you in your relationship with your family member. Speak honestly and authentically, expressing your feelings fully. This is your opportunity to speak up about the neglected or taboo areas of your relationship.

If you are bringing up an event from the past that you want to resolve, you may want to talk about what happened, how you felt—and feel—about it, how this event affected you, and what you want the person to do about it now. For the best results, avoid blaming, manipulating, or demanding. Still, feel free to express your anger, maintaining your awareness of the sensations in your body. Do this as directly and cleanly as you can. This expression of feeling is for your own healing, not to create a reaction in the other person.

Next, allow your family member to respond. Listen carefully and respectfully. Let the dialogue and interaction unfold spontaneously; don't interfere. You may find that your family member is acting different from ever before. Let this happen. Notice your own resistance to new and unfamiliar ways of relating. You may not understand what is being said. There may be nonverbal communication; there may be silence. Other things may begin to happen. The person—or your guide—may want to show you something. Be receptive to any images that appear. They may seem absurd, disturbing, or confusing, but trust that the imagination is taking you where you need to go for healing. In tapping the imagination, we gain access to a much greater knowledge than our conscious mind can grasp.

For a deeper understanding of your family member's perceptions of and feelings about your relationship, you can step inside that person's body. Look out at the world through his or her eyes. How have you been wounded? How have you struggled in this relationship? What do you want from the person (you, in your own body) standing in front of you? What do you want to say to this person? Allow a dialogue to develop between the you within the other person and the *you* relating to that person.

You may find that your meeting begins to move beyond the personal into more soulful concerns. This is not surprising, for the imagination is soul territory and, as Thomas Moore points out, relationships, particularly intensely entangled ones, can lead to the revelation of soul. He writes, "Even though we may think our strong emotions focus on the people around us, we are being set face to face with divinity itself, however we understand or speak about that mystery" (Moore, p. 257).

As your encounter with your family member comes to a close, say good-bye. If you still feel incomplete, let the person know that you will be meeting again in the imagination. Watch your family member leave, being fully aware of all that is going on inside of you. Then spend some time alone in your imaginary healing place reflecting on what has happened and on how you feel now. How have your feelings changed toward this person? Relax and absorb the healing in this place—in your imagination, lie down in the grass, bathe in a waterfall or spring, swim in the ocean, feast on a meal, climb into a warm bed.

When you open your eyes, record your experience in your journal to help you integrate it. In the following days and weeks, notice any changes that manifest in your relationship. As you clear away the inner barriers to change and transformation, you may find that you feel differently about and relate differently to this person. Explore ways you can act to support these changes. You may choose to talk with the person directly about some of the issues you explored in your imagination. Again, don't make assumptions about how he or she will react to you. Be open and receptive.

When Liana first tried this exercise in a therapy session, she was amazed by the intensity of anger she felt and expressed toward her mother. She spoke of hurts and disappointments she had never expressed before. She was experiencing those very freedoms that Satir identifies as essential to healthy family relationships: the freedom to say what she thought and felt and to take risks for herself. In the exercise, her mother simply listened; she didn't interrupt, break down in tears, or give excuses. She nodded and listened intently, as though she understood. Feeling her mother had heard her, Liana felt so much love and tenderness after their internal encounter that she reached out to her mother and hugged her. As she held her mother, she could feel her mother's heart beating close to her own.

The next time Liana performed this exercise, her mother spoke to her, sharing the concerns and difficulties that she had experienced as a mother and wife. It was a breakthrough for Liana to step inside her mother and experience the relationship through *her* eyes. She realized then how much her mother loved and cared for her. She understood how her mother's childhood wounds had crippled her emotionally, making it difficult for her to express love without narcissism or criticism.

Exercise 7-2
AN EXTERNAL ENCOUNTER

Once you have worked with internal communication to the point that you feel clear and compassionate, you can move on to external communication. First, assess your readiness by answering the following questions:

- Am I clear about what I want in this relationship?
- Do I still feel upset about the issues I addressed using internal communication?

• Am I able to speak out truthfully and listen respectfully?
• Am I able to open to the other person's point of view?

Take some time to reflect on the areas of difficulty you have with your family member. Ask yourself, "What past or present issues are inhibiting a clear, close, and respectful relationship? Where do I stand on these issues? What do I want? What do I want to change? What part have I played?"

Then set up a time to talk with the person, not in your imagination but face-to-face. When you sit down together, make your intention clear. It will build cooperation if the other person knows what benefits you hope both of you can derive from this discussion: "I want to be able to have a closer relationship with you, but these are the issues that get in my way.... It's out of my love for you and my hopes for a healthier relationship that I'm talking to you now." Then focus on one event or issue, covering these three important points:

1. This is what happened.
2. This is how I felt about it at the time.
3. This is what I want from you now.

Ask the person merely to listen to all three points without responding, agreeing, or disagreeing. With no criticism or blame, state the issue, trying to be as clear, brief, and specific as possible. Speak about your own experience and feelings, using as many "I" statements as you can.

Then ask the person to reflect on what you've said to make sure your message has come across accurately and clearly.

It is important to understand that such discussions can indeed create breakthroughs but that substantial changes in a relationship must come out of thoughtful assessment followed by small steps and clear and consistent statements and actions. One talk will not necessarily create lasting change; consistent action will. In that vein, when she felt clear about the issues she wanted to discuss with her mother, Liana had several talks with her mother using the format described above. She was able to communicate these concerns without blaming or intimidating her mother.

> In our talks, we were able to discuss the issues in our relationship that had been bothering me, particularly ones from my childhood. As we talked openly with each other, I began to see her as a person, not just as my mother. I realize now how much I kept her in the role of a mother. Since she constantly fell short of my ideal mother, I felt resentment and anger toward her for not being perfect. Once I was able to see her as a human being who had gone through her own struggles and had grown up along with us as a mother, we had some interesting conversations about her marriage, the status of women at the time of my childhood, and how these larger social issues affected her mothering. I was able to see my mother as a human being, and this helped me have compassion and understanding for her. We share our human struggles, not just our struggles as mother and daughter.

Carl Jung once wrote that until we see our parents as people with their own wounds, limitations, and failures, we are unable to grow up. When we can forgive our parents as human beings, then we can release the past and accept our parents without trying to change them. Liana discovered that this new understanding and compassion for her mother brought about a deeper and more functional relationship between them.

Many find that part of healing the relationship with a living parent involves separating expectations and inevitable disappointments from reality. Deep inside each of us we hold an image of who we want our parents to be; these images often have an archetypal origin. A flesh-and-blood parent can never measure up to these images, but our expectations and hopes often blind us to that reality. But in beginning to acknowledge the relationship as it is, we can come to appreciate what our parents have given us and to accept what they haven't.

By the way, if your family member is unwilling to accept your invitation to talk, consider writing a letter. This can be a nonthreatening way to reach out, giving the recipient time to absorb the contents without the pressure to respond immediately. Meanwhile, by continuing to work with internal communication, you may be able to influence the person's receptivity to talking and help you make peace with the relationship as it is.

Exercise 7-3
FAMILY MEETINGS

New responsibilities and roles often rise up within a family when one member begins to die. As a result, resentments can surface about contributions of time, energy, and money. Regular family meetings can be useful throughout the illness and periodically during the months of grief to discuss and work out issues, divide up responsibilities, and explore new roles with one another. This exercise will help to keep channels of communication clear.

- Set a regular time for meeting and appoint one person, preferably a different person each time, to be a timekeeper and to help keep the discussion on track.
- Use a "talking stick"—a stick, stone, flower, or other object— and pass it to each person in turn. Whoever holds the stick may speak without being interrupted while the others listen with full attention. In this way, each person updates the rest on what he or she has been going through since the last meeting.
- Follow up on issues that were discussed in the last meeting. Which decisions were implemented and which were not? Are there still some unresolved feelings about issues that were discussed?

- Write down current issues of concern.
- Brainstorm possible solutions and strategies. In this phase it is important not to edit or judge any ideas. Write them all down.
- Agree on one strategy for each issue and divide up responsibilities among family members for carrying out tasks.
- Go around the circle so that each person can express appreciation or admiration for each of the other family members present.
- Set a date for the next meeting. Then close the meeting with a prayer, blessing, poem, or song. Family members can take turns bringing an idea for closing the meeting.

Since the dying of a family member puts considerable stress on the family, disagreements and fights are common—though often unexpected. When outer communication breaks down, you can use your imagination to meet the family member in a healing place and talk about the issues that have been troubling the relationship. Internal communication techniques can help you work through difficult issues and heal old hurts. As you strengthen your imagination, you will increase your capacity to put yourself into the thoughts and feelings of others, thereby promoting compassion and respect for differences and fostering clear and effective external communication within the family.

8

Reaching Your Living Partner

I am sure of nothing but the holiness of the heart's affections
and the truth of the imagination.
John Keats

The illness and dying of a family member can also put tremendous strain on a marriage or partnership, making new demands of time, attention, and money. While one partner is attending to the dying person, the other partner may well feel abandoned and left out. And in response, the partner making the effort and doing the work may feel unsupported and misunderstood. When the family member dies, though the partners now expect relief of the tensions on their marriage, they may find a whole new set of stresses in place. As I have shown, grieving is an intensely emotional and unstable time. Exhausted after a prolonged period of caring for a dying family member, the griever may now have the additional stress of caring for survivors who are also grieving. There is often little energy left over for a partner.

Furthermore, the "outsider" may feel overwhelmed by the intensity of the other's grief. Particularly if he or she has not yet experienced the death of a family member, this person may just not understand the intensity of the experience. The nongrieving partner may see confusing—even alarming—and rapid changes in the grieving partner and ask, "Who *is* this person? This seems like a stranger, not the person I married at all." Nevertheless, changes in one partner will necessitate changes in the relationship, whether or not the other partner is willing to make them. Understandably, the need to work at change can trigger resentment for the other partner.

When both partners are grieving, it would seem that things would be easier because there is common ground, but this is not necessarily so. For example, a partner may be grieving a beloved mother- or father-in-law, the death of whom may be as hard or harder than that of one's own parent. However, this grief may be seen as less significant by the other partner or family members. The partner who has lost a sibling or parent may feel resentful that the other partner is grieving and not giving needed support.

The loss of a child creates incredible stress for both parents and for the marriage. Grief symptoms are usually more intense and last longer as parents struggle with complex issues: They have lost a part of themselves along with their identity as parents, their dreams for the future have been devastated, a natural order of life has been violated, and they are often beset with guilt and anger for not being able to protect their child. Just when partners need the support of one another, both are grieving and incapable of providing that support. The closeness that is usually a strength in a marriage can actually be a liability after the loss of a child. Since it is common for people in this situation to displace the anger and guilt on those who are closest, often it is the spouse who is the recipient of these feelings.

It may be difficult for either partner to pull away in order to get some solitary time to heal, reflect, or just take a break from the grief. There can also be tensions if one partner expects the other to grieve in a certain way. Mothers and fathers grieve differently over time. Each parent will have had a unique relationship with that child, and so the grief will be different.

Moreover, partners may deal with such stresses differently owing to cultural differences, family conditioning, and birth order. So the effects of the death spiral on and on, and disagreements are common.

In the midst of their family loss, couples tend to downplay more often than not the extent of the stress it places on their partnership. They may not even recognize that the escalation of fights or tension has its underlying source in grief. This is particularly true in the months of grief after the immediate crisis of the illness and dying has passed. At that time, those in grief often feel pressure from partners, friends, and other family members to "snap out of it" and get on with their lives. And yet the grieving process goes on and on, shaking up partnerships and initiating intensive change.

Surviving Turbulence

In response to the changes in the grieving person, many partners in intimate relationships can expect to go through a period of turbulence. Just as in other areas of life during this time, issues that have been simmering under the surface may come up; compromises that have been tolerated for years may suddenly become intolerable. Both partners might see unhealthy patterns in the relationship with increased clarity, and particularly the grieving partner may be less likely to tolerate these patterns than before. Some marriages and partnerships grow apart and split up under these new pressures. Many of my clients have confirmed that their partners' lack of support through such a major and difficult life event was a major factor in their decision to terminate a marriage or relationship.

If a marriage or partnership is going to survive this difficult time, communication is critical. As with Liana and her husband, many couples find that, at the very time they most need to, they are unable to talk with one another in a meaningful and supportive way. At the beginning of a relationship, most partners feel that they can talk with their mates freely and honestly. However, over time hurts and misunderstandings accumulate; unrealistic expectations produce disappointments. With so much at stake, partners tend to hide their vulnerability and needs, mask their anger, and avoid discussion of sensitive issues. Unexpressed feelings then find expression in distorted ways—for example, in explosions of anger, repetitive arguments, and sarcastic and belittling comments.

This breakdown in communication becomes critical when one or both partners are grieving and desperately need the other person's understanding and support.

The good news, again, is that internal communication techniques can be highly effective in breaking through damaging patterns of communication and working through old hurts which are currently affecting the relationship. The imagery exercises in chapter 6 are useful in this context; also, letter writing—you write to your partner *and* create a response, all without "sending" the letters—is a nonconfrontational way of working through difficult feelings. I recommend using the format that John Gray describes in *Men Are from Mars, Women Are from Venus*. He suggests first writing a Love Letter that expresses your feelings of love as well as anger, sadness, and regret about the relationship. Write it as though your partner were open to hearing what you have to say. Next, write a Response Letter, a reply from your partner's point of view. Include in this letter whatever you wish to hear from your partner in the way of acknowledgment, understanding, and support. Writing these letters will give you the opportunity to express what you think, feel, and want. You'll also learn to listen to yourself, since you'll be writing a letter of acknowledgment back to yourself. Once you are able not only to express yourself openly and honestly but also to honor that expression, you will be much more likely to feel yourself heard and supported by your partner. Though the exercise does not require it, you may indeed decide to share these letters with your partner to help him or her better understand your needs.

Once you have voiced unexpressed feelings and gained more understanding and compassion, then an actual exchange of letters between partners may be helpful in rebuilding trust and intimacy. Writing and actually delivering letters to one another can help each partner explore and express feelings and concerns in a safe way. Receiving letters can help each partner take in and reflect on the concerns of the other without the pressure of having to respond immediately. This gives a partner necessary feedback and shows where change is needed. Each partner can read and reflect on what has been written, learn what is important to the other, and decide what he or she can do to support the other person.

The following exercise is for both partners.

Exercise 8-1
WRITING A GRIEF LETTER TO YOUR PARTNER/SPOUSE

Write a letter to your partner, focusing on how grief has affected and changed your partnership. Go into separate rooms and write your letters, being as honest and open as you can. Focus on your feelings and concerns.

If you are the grieving partner, write about your experience of grieving:

- What has been difficult for you?
- What are your fears?
- What have you appreciated about your partner?
- What have you resented or regretted?
- What do you want from your partner?
- Do you feel your partner has supported you?
- If not, what could he or she do to better support you?
- Have any new realizations or understandings come out of your grief?
- What patterns in your relationship do you see more clearly now?
- What changes do you want to make in your relationship?

If you are the nongrieving partner, write about how it has been for you to live with a person who is grieving:

- What has been difficult or challenging for you?
- How have you felt about the changes you've seen in your partner?
- Have you felt left out or abandoned?
- Have you felt appreciated for your efforts to support your partner through this crisis?

• What do you now appreciate, fear, or regret?
• What do you want from your partner?
• What are your visions of the future?

In both cases, write as though your partner were listening with love and understanding. Take the risk of sharing feelings and thoughts that you ordinarily hold back. Try to focus on your own experience rather than blaming or judging your partner.

When you've both finished your letters, exchange them. Take your time to read your partner's letter, reflecting on what has been expressed. You can either write a response or sit down together to talk about your responses.

Once you have written letters in this manner, assess your readiness to talk with your partner, as you did with members of your family of origin:

• Am I able to speak out truthfully as well as listen respectfully?
• Am I able to understand the other person's point of view?
• Do I still feel upset about the issues I addressed in my letter?
• Am I clear about what I want in my relationship?

Six months after the death of Liana's father, Liana and Tim's marriage was suffering from a year of neglect, lack of communication, and tumultuous emotions. The year before her father had died, Liana had been frequently away from home while caring for him. Even though he understood her concerns for her father, Tim felt pushed away and abandoned. His hopes that their marriage would return to normal after the death were not realized; her grief seemed to go on and on and the intensity of it was often overwhelming to him. Liana, on the other hand, felt lonely and unsupported. Every time she tried to talk to Tim about her concerns, the discussion ended up in a fight; neither person felt understood or heard.

In an effort to establish communication again, Liana and Tim agreed to write letters to one another.

After exchanging these letters, Tim and Liana felt more understanding. Tim learned that all he had to do was listen. It was a revelation to him that he didn't have to "make his wife feel better." After writing her letter, Liana realized that she had experienced the same feelings of abandonment with her father that she now felt with her husband. This made her wonder whether some of her current anger and disappointment wasn't a carryover from her relationship with her father in adolescence. To explore this possibility further, Liana decided to work on her relationship with her father using internal communication (see chapter 4). A few weeks later, Tim and Liana felt ready to sit down and talk with one another about the issues they had previously been avoiding. This time each of them was able to speak about current concerns in their relationship and to listen to the other respectfully. Their dialogue that continued over months enriched their relationship and helped them both mature as marriage partners.

An important part of the grieving period are weekly talks in which each person can voice concerns, resentments, and appreciations; discuss what is and isn't working; and explore solutions. Such talks can build intimacy and provide the space for partners to explore creative solutions to new demands and problems. They also keep resentments from building up. In *The New Peoplemaking*, Virginia Satir writes, "Once a human being has arrived on this earth, communication is the largest single factor determining what kinds of relationships she or he makes with others and what happens to each in the world" (Satir, p. 51).

With the death of a loved one, many issues regarding life's meaning may suddenly intrude themselves into daily life: what you must do to die in peace; what gives purpose and meaning to life; what hopes, fears, and dreams you harbor; what it means to live fully and authentically; how you are related to the infinite. The philosopher Friedrich Nietzsche called marriage a grand conversation (Nietzsche, p. 59). Although a loss puts tremendous stress on a partnership, often in a sudden and unexpected way, confronting and responding to this major crisis allows a dialogue to open that can renew and deepen the relationship and enrich both partners.

Equally important is taking quiet time for yourself. One possibility, as I have discussed before, is creating a sanctuary where you can go to grieve, reflect, and regenerate. Your sanctuary could be in your home or in nature or wherever you are able to open fully to your grief for at least fifteen minutes a day. This is a time to give yourself nurturance, love, encouragement, and protection. It is also a time to explore and express the feelings and thoughts that are surfacing, to resolve unfinished business with the deceased, and to work on issues arising with your partner and other family members.

In my sanctuary, I meditated, prayed, wrote in my journal, recorded my dreams, cried, or just sat and looked at my father's picture. This place became a womb that cradled me in my grief, a refuge where I could embrace the pain and acknowledge the power and impact of this passage in my life. By focusing full attention on my grief for small interludes each day, I became more present for my husband. Seeing that I was actively taking care of myself, he felt less pressured to help me cope with my grief. He then could give me the gift of his caring presence. On the nights I cried myself to sleep, he simply held me close. He didn't feel the need to say anything to try to make me feel better. Many people complain that their partners cannot just be with them when they are in pain. Those partners want to "fix" the problem. I encourage my clients to communicate to their partners that it is enough just to be with a loved one as he or she is crying or feels sad.

The Positive Impact of a Death

After the death of a loved one, partners are likely to take marriage much more seriously. They realize in a concrete way that time is limited, life is precious, and love is more important than anything else.

Chris and Rebecca both lost their fathers suddenly to heart attacks, Rebecca's two years before Chris's. As is often the case, the first death was the most difficult for their marriage, because Chris did not really understand what Rebecca was going through. With the second death, their shared experience of loss drew them closer and helped resolve the earlier misunderstandings. Here is Chris's account of this deep and productive inner change:

> I've gone through two major events of my life with Rebecca: my father's death and sobriety. I don't know what it would have been like to do these two things without her. In my worst moments I'll think I couldn't have done it without her, but in my better moments I think I'm lucky and fortunate that I did have someone to help me through these things. With the death of our fathers, it was moving-up day. We weren't kids anymore. We were now our parents' generation. Becoming the generation that's in the middle, that takes care of the older and the younger people, broke a barrier for me. When her father died, I understood for the first time one of the reasons people have children. I suddenly realized what it would be to be alone.

Chris and Rebecca both appreciated the fact that, in the face of the devastating loss of a parent, the companionship and support of a partner are priceless. They each expressed faith in their partner's ability to come through for them in the future. Every spouse wonders whether the partner will really be there at a time of great crisis, and the death of a parent can be the first major test of this question. If a partner *does* pass this test, a great infusion of confidence in the relationship can help both people move through the challenges and losses of midlife.

With this awareness, many people have set out to challenge the conditioning that holds them back from the loving and supportive relationships that they want and deserve. The death of Robin's parents impelled her to reevaluate her understanding of marriage and relationship—versions that she had inherited from her parents.

> It wasn't just burying these two individuals who raised me and protected me and had been there every breathing minute that I had walked this earth. I buried my childhood. I buried all sense of a connection to human beings that had any history on me. I also buried my parents' marriage. My parents' deaths helped me see who my parents were as individuals—how they related to one another, how my mother saw herself as a woman, how my father saw her as a woman. I began to clarify what concepts I inherited from them and what were really my own.

As Robin's comments demonstrate, the death of a parent can dramatically increase awareness of parental conditioning and its effect on one's own marriage. Parental expectations as well as the difficulties and patterns in the parents' relationship can unconsciously and insidiously affect the formation of similar patterns in one's own marriage or intimate relationship. It can be a rude shock to wake up to and see clearly how much like one's parents one has become—despite efforts to move in the opposite direction. The definitive separation from a parent through death can free the adult child to challenge the conditioning that may have set a blueprint for the relationship.

Ray, whose letter to her father appears earlier, observed that she was living out the relationship with her partner in the same way that her father had lived with her mother:

> My father's death made me realize that I had been living out my relationship with my partner exactly as my father lived out his relationship with my mother—don't rock the boat, just live your

life side by side, but don't ever ask or expect anything. My mother's partner was obsessed with his work, as my partner is.

As she gained insight into this pattern, Ray stopped to ask, "Is this what I really want in my relationship?" She wanted a very different kind of relationship, one in which she could be fully expressive of her passions and needs, one in which she could shine. She was going to have to rock the boat in order to instigate these changes, a prospect that both frightened and excited her.

As you deepen and transform your relationship with a partner through communication—both internal and external—you may discover that an intimate partnership is not just a coming together of two individuals but the mysterious formation of a third entity, one that is greater than either individual can be separately and that invites both of you to grow and to expand beyond your individual limitations.

Suggestions for Partners

· Remind each other repeatedly that grief creates considerable stress in your partnership/marriage. Escalation of fights and tension are common.

· If you are the nongrieving partner, educate yourself about what your partner is going through: talk to others about grief, read, and listen to tapes to learn whatever you can about the nature and timing of grief. Understand that people grieve in different ways.

· Actively commit to communicate with one another. Set aside specific times to talk, exploring how you are supporting one another, what you need from one another, and how the grief is affecting the relationship. It may be helpful to write one another a Grief Letter (see exercise 8-1).

· If communication has broken down between you or if you feel too vulnerable and raw to communicate directly with your partner, consider internal communication techniques, such as the imagery exercises in chapter 6 or the letter-writing activity discussed in chapter 4.

· Take time for yourself without feeling guilty for withdrawing. You need solitary time for reflection and healing. You also may need to take a break from grieving.

· Look at the issues that surface in your marriage—resentments, walls between you, compromises that have become intolerable, unhealthy conditioned responses that go back to your parents' relationship.

· Use grief as an opportunity to be more vulnerable and open with one another. Grief opens hearts.

· Review from time to time the daily losses your relationship has encountered. Have these losses been acknowledged, grieved, and integrated into the marriage? Some losses may need additional healing—perhaps a miscarriage or infidelity. Consider doing a ritual that acknowledges this loss and helps you both let go. You also may want to draw a loss timeline (see chapter 12) to get an overall perspective of the presence of loss in your relationship.

· Acknowledge that grief will change you and your relationship; take time with your partner to identify what you both want in your marriage/partnership.

9

Reaching Your Living Children

*Kids are the best teachers of life's most profound spiritual lessons: that pain
and suffering are as much a part of life as happiness and joy; that change
and impermanence are all we can count on for sure; that we don't
really run the show; and that if we can't find the maturity to surrender to
these difficult truths, we'll always be unhappy that our lives—and our
children's—aren't turning out the way we expected or planned.*

Harriet Lerner

During a family member's illness or decline, one's children may feel upset
by a decrease in attention, by changes in routines, by the heightened emotions of the adults around them, or by their own grief. They may feel frightened by turmoil around the illness or threatened by tension in the
household as the marriage is tested by the increased stress and demands.

Talking with My Son about Death

My son began acting out soon after I received the news of my father's cancer. The more preoccupied I became, the louder he yelled and the more he
tested. Keeping my father's secret, I had not told my son about his grandfather's illness. I had shared the news only with my husband. But with the
escalating situation with my son, I realized that I could not subject my
family to my father's rules. I, like many struggling to cope with the stress
of a parent's illness, had fallen back into the unhealthy patterns I had
learned as a child. My parents' method of coping with their crisis was not
healthy for my family. The secret was festering inside me and my son was
sensing this, as children do. Carl Jung wrote, "The *participation mystique,*

157

that is, the primitive unconscious identity of the child with its parents, causes the child to feel the conflicts of the parents, and to suffer from them as though they were its own troubles. It is hardly ever the open conflict of the manifest difficulty that has the poisonous effect; it is almost always a disharmony repressed and neglected by the parents" (Wickes, p. 36).

I began talking with my son about my father's illness. At this point, my son responded more to my sadness than to his grandfather's illness. Seeing no physical changes in his grandfather, the cancer was not real to him yet. I told a few close friends as well. I could breathe fully again. And my son calmed down.

I knew that the road ahead would be very hard, but I now felt that I had the support of my family and friends. Most of all, in speaking out I had acknowledged to myself how big an event this was in my life. One of the two people who had given me life was now dying, creating momentous shifts inside me. Suddenly there was no more buffer between me and death. I was next. This propelled me into a painful evaluation of what really mattered in my life. I saw what was important to my father as his life came to a close. He had lived for his work, but now all the accomplishments, money, and medals seemed insignificant to him. Only love remained. I felt a new appreciation for my family and loved ones, realizing the preciousness of simple moments with them.

Richard Byrd wrote in a letter to his family when he thought he was dying at the South Pole, "I saw my whole life pass in review. I realized how wrong my sense of values had been and how I had failed to see that the simple, homely, unpretentious things of life are the most important. . . . Only two things matter to a man and they are affection and understanding of his family. Every thing else he creates are insubstantial but the family is an everlasting anchorage (Byrd, pp. 178–79).

The loss of a loved one can deepen parents' appreciation of their children—even when they consider it impossible to cherish the children more than they do. Many parents who experience a loss not only value their time with their children more afterward but also feel a new urgency about improving the quality of their parenting. One of my clients told me that six months after the death of his mother, "My relationships with my children are so much more important to me. . . . Now that I realize how quickly my time with them will pass, I feel a strong commitment to spending more quality time with them, expressing my appreciation of them as individuals, and healing the wounds I have created in our relationship through my own conditioning and negligence. I have been looking at all the ways I have parented them that have divided us rather than brought us closer."

Finding a Balance between Grieving and Parenting

Even with this awareness, I was often drained to the point of exhaustion and therefore unable to give my family the care and presence that I wanted to. Establishing some way of regenerating myself in the midst of family demands became a critical task. As I have discussed before, I created a sanctuary where I could go to reflect, grieve, and regenerate. As I used the sanctuary every day, I felt better prepared to step back into my family and into the world. By focusing full attention on my grief for even brief periods each day, I was more able to be present for my family, clients, and friends. I could attend to daily routines and commitments without feeling distracted or overwhelmed. At a time when my inner life was so chaotic and unpredictable, it was comforting in fact to partake in daily tasks.

My son responded well to this change. He felt less threatened by my vulnerable emotional state. He expressed concern and interest in my father's illness, asking many questions. He realized that I too could become ill and die. We had many talks about this in our quiet time before bed.

Helping Our Children Grieve

Once we are grounded in our own grief, we are less likely to overwhelm our children with our own grief. We are able to be more present for them and to their concerns, for this is often a confusing, even frightening time for children. For some it is their first experience of the death of a loved one. Give your children permission to grieve and prepare them for what they might experience while grieving. They need to know that they might feel sad for a while. Help them express their feelings in ways that are natural and safe for them, perhaps through play. It is important to talk with them about what is happening in the family, to be responsive to their questions and concerns, and to prepare them for the changes— whether in routine, in their parent's emotional state, or in the progression of the illness.

I shared with my son that I was feeling very raw and emotional as my dad was dying, that he would see me express strong feelings from time to time. I let him know that I was OK when I cried, that it helped me heal. I asked him to let me know whenever he was feeling uncomfortable. I also shared with him the changes to expect each time we saw his grandfather. By this time, my father was declining rapidly in the hospital.

The hospital was two hours away from my home. I visited Dad as often as I could, but I wanted to be with him more. I knew that my time with him was running out. I also wanted to support my mother in her hospital vigil, as she was under great pressure making daily medical decisions. However, since my husband commuted to work, I had primary responsibility for our son during the day in addition to my psychotherapy practice. To go to the hospital during the week involved complicated arrangements for my son and rescheduling of clients. I felt pulled to be with Dad, without the flexibility to respond as I wanted to.

On the weekends, I often went to the hospital with my husband. I appreciated his support and company on the long drive, especially on the way home when I was very emotional. Each time I left my father at the hospital, I wept, knowing that this could be the last time I saw him.

We gave our son the choice of whether he wanted to come or not, sharing with him some of the changes he would see in his granddad since his last visit. On the first weekend, my son responded, "No, I don't want to go. I think it would be too sad." He went to visit his other grandparents that day. The next day he requested to see his grandfather.

As he entered the hospital room, his vitality and energy sharply contrasted with the sterile environment. He was at first taken aback by his grandfather's expression, eyes half open but unseeing, the pallor of his unshaved cheeks, the raspy breathing. "He looks so old," he said, looking to us for assurance. Seeing that we were not alarmed but accepting of the situation, he began exploring. "Can Granddad hear me if I talk to him?" I told him that we don't know what people experience when they are in a coma but there is a good possibility that a person still has some awareness of sound. My son proceeded to tell his grandfather all about his day. Then he checked out the equipment that my father was attached to, asking many questions of the nurses.

By the time we left, he told me that he was glad he had visited with his grandfather. That night, he drew a picture of the hospital, instructing me to draw Granddad in the bed while he drew the family gathered around. Then he drew a wavy-lined shape near the ceiling. "This is Granddad's spirit," he said, "looking down on everything."

Bringing Death Back into the Family

It is important to bring children into the hospital and into the rooms of the dying—when they express a desire to. It is important to take the time for their questions and encourage their investigation into death. We each have our own ideas about death, but it is helpful to acknowledge that no one really knows what happens after death and to make room for our children to explore their own ideas. Their fresh perspectives can be a learning for everyone. Death needs to be brought back into the family.

Before the technological revolution, people died at home, cared for by the family and the family doctor, who were present at the births as well. Death was accepted as part of the cycle of life. Children had the opportunity to come to terms with death. They participated in caring for the dying; they saw dead bodies. Death was not a stranger. But as people began dying in hospitals, the situation changed dramatically. Dying was no longer an integral part of family life.

Some of my clients who lost a parent or grandparent in childhood have shared how adults tried to protect them from the situation, which only resulted in increased anxiety and confusion. Many were not allowed, even when they asked, to enter the sickroom or see the dead body. Talk about the event was discouraged. In some cases the children were quickly whisked away to another environment. In being protected from death and grief, they had no opportunity to resolve their feelings or to experience death as a part of the natural cycle of life.

I was not with my father when he died. It seemed significant that although I wanted to be perfectly in tune with his passing, I was in the midst of my duties as a mother. I was waiting for the dentist to fill the seven cavities that had suddenly sprouted in my son's mouth. I felt impatient that it was taking so long when my father was dying. I wanted to be at home, meditating and praying. I had found that in my sanctuary, I felt closer to Dad than I did in the hospital room, especially once he sank into a coma. Closing my eyes, I could talk to him through my heart or access clear images of him in an inner world.

Receiving my mother's phone call that Dad had just died in her arms, I was thrust into a deeper level of grief. The finality was frightening. I would never see my father again. My heart felt at times that it was splitting open from the pain. I felt full of sorrow and confusion and also of joy and gratitude. I had never felt so alone—or so grown up. I had become a different woman, a woman without a father. With the labor of giving birth to my son, I had discovered a source of power within me that was beyond my previous concepts. With my father's death, the woman in me stepped out with a new freedom to express that power and to take charge of my parenting and my life.

A bereavement period, then, can be a time when one takes parenting into one's own hands. Looking at how their parenting has been influenced by their own parents' advice and agendas, parents can begin to redefine parenting from their own values and standards.

Letting Go

Parenting involves a delicate dance of close connection and separation. In reaction to the loss of a family member, we may tend to hold on tighter to our children. However, as we let go of a deceased loved one, we must also learn to let our children go. Remembering our own struggles to separate from our parents, we can appreciate our children's struggle to separate from us. We must let go so they can become themselves.

Natural developments aid in the letting-go process. The loss of a family member can help us see and honor a child as an individual rather than as an extension of ourselves or of our family. Many parents unconsciously live out their own ambitions and dreams through their children—it was for this reason that Carl Jung wrote that the unlived life of the parent is the child's greatest burden. However, the awakening to one's own life that typically occurs after the loss of a parent can actually free children to be themselves and to explore their own unique paths.

Consider Jacqueline, who struggled with the spirited nature of her daughter from the moment the girl was born. Jacqueline herself had been conditioned to be "a nice girl," and she unconsciously expected her very feisty daughter to conform to the rules as well. But when her mother died, Jacqueline felt freed to explore her *own* feistiness, and as a result she came to respect and honor this quality in her daughter. This changed her relationship with her daughter—suddenly she could relax and enjoy her.

The whole constellation moves in a different way. My parents' myth of being nice—not asking too much, hoping for the best, and then being secretly fuming if you don't get it—has shifted. Now there's open space for that story to be rewritten. . . . Being nice is not one of my daughter's struggles, never was and never will be. My mother tried to tame my spirit. I wasn't a nice little girl with bows in my hair, and I couldn't be. Neither is my daughter. I can actualize my daughter's strength so much more.

Integrating the Truth

Just as a death in the family can affect a parent's perception of his or her child, so it can alter a child's perspective on life and death. When this happens, it is important for the parent-child relationship to serve as a sanctuary for the child where he or she can explore and integrate new awarenesses. As children watch a family member die or a parent grieve, they may feel frightened at the prospect of other family members dying. One four-year-old who witnessed both her father's death and that of a family friend asked, "Why are there so many deaths? Am I going to die? Are you?" It is important to listen to your children's concerns and to take time to explore their questions.

A child's first exposure to death is often accompanied by a period of moodiness and instability while the child struggles to integrate the awareness that loved ones do in fact die. The awareness of the fragility of life and the certainty of death can make parents appreciate the relationship with their children—and children with their parents—even more than before.

Young children often have difficulty expressing to their parents what it is that troubles them about the death of someone close to them. Exercise 9-1 gives children the opportunity to confront their problems in symbolic language and to gain help and guidance from their imaginations. They can express their feelings and concerns to the people and animals they meet in their imaginations, dialogue with them, and learn new ways of coping from them.

Fairy Tales

Fairy tales are healing to both adults and children. In *The Uses of Enchantment*, Bruno Bettelheim writes, "Each fairy tale is a magic mirror which reflects some aspects of our inner world. . . . For those who immerse themselves in what the fairy tale has to communicate, it becomes a deep, quiet pool which at first seems to reflect only our own image; but behind it we soon discover the inner turmoils of our soul—its depth, and ways to gain peace within ourselves and with the world, which is the reward of our struggles" (Bettelheim, p. 309). The people of fairy tales confront suffering, hardship, trials, isolation, abandonment, and loss. Each person finds help and guidance; each finds a way through the ordeals, attaining love, happiness, wisdom, or riches. Fairy tales assure us that when we struggle against the inevitable difficulties of life such as the loss of a loved one, we can turn to the imagination for the resources we need to heal and go on with our lives.

Fairy tales teach us that in the imagination things are often other than what they seem—a kind grandmother may be a hungry wolf, an ugly frog may be a charming prince, a gift may be a curse. Even death may not be the ending we take it to be. In many fairy tales, death is not the end of the story or the end of a life. A person can be dead at one point in the story and then restored to life at a later one. Snow White's death is mourned by those who love her, but she comes back to life—even more beautiful than she had been. Little Red Riding Hood leaps out of the wolf's belly transformed into a mature maiden. In reading and rereading fairy tales, we learn to prepare ourselves for the new beginnings, unexpected events, and transformations hidden within death.

Exercise 9-1
WRITING A FAIRY TALE

Create a stack of index cards with the names of places, animals and other creatures, magical beings, magical objects, and people (see the groupings below for suggestions). Then place these cards face down in stacks, one for each category. Choose a time, such as bedtime, and create an environment that is conducive to storytelling. Ensure that you will not be interrupted. Close the door, light a candle, and gather special toys around the bed. Invite your child to choose one card randomly from each of the five stacks. Reading each one out loud, lay the chosen cards before you both.

Ask your child to start with the magical opening "Once upon a time" and tell you a fairy tale that features these five words. Encourage your child to use the words in any order and to add any other words desired. If your child expresses doubts about being able to create a fairy tale, assure him or her that the fairy tale, once started, will soon begin to tell itself.

An older child may choose to write the fairy tale rather than tell it out loud. Then one of you can read it out loud to the other.

When the fairy tale is finished, ask your child to give it a title. Your child might also illustrate the fairy tale and then create a small book.

Take some time to reflect on your child's fairy tale. What is the central challenge or test in the story? What form does help or guidance take? How does the central character overcome adversity, and how is that character strengthened by these ordeals? Does the fairy tale reflect your child's inner conflicts or anxieties? Does the fairy tale inspire new perspectives and insights? Did you observe any changes in your child after the fairy tale was written? If so, what changes? How can you support any growth or new perspectives that your child's fairy tale inspired?

- *Places*: Mountain, bazaar, sea, valley, pool, lake, desert, castle, mountain pass, village, cave, tunnel, meadow, tree, garden, forest, fire, dungeon, church, bridge, city, crossroads, fountain, hollow, island, palace, river, ship, temple, tower, volcano, wall, door, house, spring

- *Animals and other creatures*: Turtle, raven, worm, serpent, dove, whale, horse, fish, sparrow, crane, camel, lamb, rat, owl, frog, swan, fox, crocodile, dog, cat, swallow, bear, lion, eagle, monkey, bee, pig, dolphin, peacock, ox, hare, lion, cock, wolf, bull, butterfly, crow, dove, elephant, leopard, spider, stag, vulture, hawk
- *Magical beings*: Unicorn, dragon, troll, giant, fairy, goblin, mermaid, angel, sorceress, dwarf, monster, wizard, soothsayer, fairy godmother, phoenix, centaur, griffin, trickster, shaman
- *Magical objects*: Egg, gold, cauldron, ring, ivory, stone, crown, shell, cross, treasure, seed, chalice, drum, star, horn, anchor, pearl, bell, arrow, ladder, sword, rose, book, ax, bone, bow, candle, cloak, crystal, diamond, feather, fire, flute, goblet, chalice, grail, helmet, herbs, jewel, key, lamp, lyre, mask, mirror, pearl, rope, veil, trident, thunderbolt, torch, thorn, moon, sun, thread
- *People*: Harpist, hermit, knight, princess, prince, queen, king, mother, father, grandmother, grandfather, musician, old man, old woman, harlot, wild man, child, clown, farmer, priest, priestess, nun, monk, maiden, carpenter, healer, girl, boy, pirate, gypsy, fool, brother, sister, virgin, twin, invalid, friend, orphan, crone

By focusing on the interaction between two brothers in his fairy tale, a six-year-old I'll call Casey was able to express and explore his feelings about the death of his older brother, which had occurred nine months before. Casey's imagination guided him right to the source of his unresolved grief—the guilt and anger that had been festering inside him for months. Since he had avoided talking about his brother's death, the fairy tale represented a breakthrough for both Casey and his mother. By reading his fairy tale, his mother was able to discover how her son was dealing with his loss. This child picked these words: *fountain*, *monster*, *twins*, *cauldron*, and *dove*. With his mother writing it down, he then created this story:

BROTHERLY LOVE

Once upon a time, in a land far, far away, there was a town. In the center of the town was a fountain. Underneath the *fountain* there lived a *monster* who only ate children and loved to eat twins.

In the town there was only one set of *twins*, John and Danny. John was the smart one, and Danny was the strong one. Now this monster was always trying to get the twins to stand over the trap door which led to his home.

One day, when John was sick, their mom sent Danny out for some medicine. Without John to warn him, Danny stood right on top of the trap door. The monster cooked him in a big *cauldron* and ate him.

When John heard of Danny's death, he asked a little *dove* to help him kill the monster. So, one day, with the dove at his side, John stood above the trap door. When the monster captured him, he told the dove to fly around the monster's head fast. When the dove was finished, the monster was so dizzy that he fell backwards into the cauldron and died.

But John's life wasn't full. He still missed Danny. One night a spirit came down from the heavens and said, "If you keep him alive in your heart, he will never die." The End.

In the opening lines of his fairy tale, Casey gives death a form he can relate to—a monster who traps and eats twin brothers. Casey then carefully delineates the revenge that brother John exacts on the monster. Although Casey had probably felt helpless watching his sick brother die, John was not powerless—he plotted a way to trick the monster and then kill him. This healing story helped Casey relive the trauma of losing his brother, express his rage toward a tangible object, and discover that his brother lives on in his heart, where he will never die.

Suggestions for Parents

- Communicate with your child about death and grief, being as honest and straightforward as your child can understand. Take the time to answer your child's questions, acknowledging what you don't know. Also, remember that children tend to interpret things literally. For example, if you tell him that his grandmother is "sleeping forever" or is "taking a long trip," he might assume that if he goes to sleep he too might sleep forever or that grandmother will return from her trip.

- Take your child's developmental stage into account; you child will not grieve as an adult does. Children do not have the same capacity as adults to tolerate intense pain over a period of time; they will grieve in spurts and may even postpone deep grieving until a later stage of development.

- Share with your child what to expect if she visits a dying family member. If your child doesn't want to go, honor her decision. Explore other ways your child can communicate with that family member—for example, talking through her heart, guided imagery, drawing a picture, or writing a letter.

- Give your child encouragement to grieve and prepare him for what he might experience while grieving—that he might feel sad or unhappy for a while. Invite him to share his feelings and questions with you and help him to express his feelings in ways that are natural and safe for him, utilizing play and the imagination.

- Include your child in funerals and memorials; it is her right to be included. Attempts to protect your child from death and grief can have long-lasting negative effects. However, don't force a child to go to a funeral if she doesn't want to. And honor her refusal to participate in any part of the ceremony—she may not, for example, want to look inside the casket or kiss the dead person.

• Attend to your own grieving. Your modeling of healthy grieving is more important than you realize. Show your child how you are taking care of yourself in your grief. Your child might want to help you create an altar for the sanctuary and, if she sees you using it regularly, might choose to use that herself from time to time.

10

Reaching Your Living Friends

Grief re-writes your address book for you.
Stephanie Ericsson

Friendships often change in quality and intensity—even quantity—after a loved one's death. With new priorities and clarified values, people who have lost someone significant to them often come to appreciate the importance of their friendships anew and come to take more responsibility for their quality. This can result in the deepening of some friendships and the letting go of others. As a family shrinks with the death of one or both parents, grandparents, and siblings, the members begin to redefine their sense of family, expanding it to embrace friends or mentors. A new appreciation may develop, too, for a living sense of community. Robin describes just such an experience:

After my parents died, my relationships started changing with women and men. I dropped the unhealthy ones while others grew healthier and deeper. I began to choose my friends more consciously. Subsequently I think I have quite an array of friends. I've never felt more loved in my entire life. I read a quote a while ago that said, "In the evening of our lives we will be judged on love alone." I feel so lucky that in the broad daylight of my life I know exactly what that person is saying, and love is the most important thing. I feel so much more capable of loving, not just other people, but myself.

Shifting Sands

Although a few friends might come forward with support and understanding during a time of loss, it is common too for some to back away at this critical time, intimidated by changes in grieving friends' behavior or uncomfortable with the intensity of emotions. It's not unusual for people to report that a death in the family shows who a person's real friends are.

Like Robin, Jacqueline became more discerning in the quality of her friendships after her parents died. But in contrast to Robin, she felt less inclined to spend time with her friends than before, choosing instead to spend more time with her family and by herself. This was a marked change in her life, as she had previously given priority to her friends. She told me, "I don't have the patience or the energy to go through friendships that are compromised. I'd much rather be alone than talk about superficial things."

In experiencing such shifts and changes in what you want from your friendships, it is helpful to speak out directly to tell your friends what isn't working for you—and, of course, what is. Too many people mistakenly assume that their friends perceive the friendship just as they do, and this unrecognized lack of congruence can lead to misunderstandings. Friendships that survive will go through inevitable adjustments. My friend Eileen moved to Europe a few months before I heard that my father had cancer. In the chaotic months that followed I reached out to her, but she was absorbed in helping her family adjust to a new home. No matter how hard I tried to explain to her what I was going through, she seemed unable to understand. Finally, out of desperation, I wrote and expressed my anger at her neglect at such a critical time for me. She called me immediately from Germany and from that point became much more responsive. Not having experienced the dying of a parent herself, she had had no idea of what this was like. To give the support and understanding we hope for from them, friends need to be educated about the impact of death and dying within a family.

While critical issues may surface in a friendship after the death of a loved one, a person in grief may feel too overwhelmed to explore these issues in person. In such cases, internal communication can help take the pressure off and provide some sense of resolution until the person feels ready to communicate outwardly.

Sometimes the person who has lost a loved one feels too raw and vulnerable to risk rejection. One of my clients, Gloria, told me that after her mother's death she stopped reaching out to her friends and stopped returning their calls, a dramatic change in her behavior. Also, she felt lonely and disturbed by the fights that were erupting with her partner. Whereas before her mother's death she had had a broad support network, in her grief she turned solely to her partner for support and comfort. This placed enormous pressure on that one single relationship. Hence, the fights.

As we explored this situation together, Gloria discovered that she had made assumptions about friendship that now closed off her options. She believed that it was only fair that she listen equally to her friends' concerns and problems if she was going to share hers. As a result she didn't call her friends in her grief because she lacked the energy in her grief to listen to her friends' problems. We talked about the possibility of sharing this dilemma with her friends rather than withdrawing from them. It is always critical to keep from making assumptions about what a friend wants or expects, assumptions that can hold friendships to old molds at a time when so much opportunity exists for renewal and change.

As Gloria reviewed her friendships, she identified a couple of people whom she wanted to contact. Others she chose not to contact, because she wasn't sure she wanted these friendships to continue. She chose to use internal communication exercises in my office to express her anger and disappointment in their reactions to her grief. Working through old hurts in this way helped her feel more at peace.

As they watch their loved ones die, many people come to realize in a new and concrete way just how important friends and family are; they understand that they want love in their lives and don't want to die in loneliness.

Ray explains how her father's lonely death made her want to deepen her friendships by sharing more meaningful experiences with them:

> Even though we were there touching him and taking care of him, my father still had a lonely death, because he had been lonely his whole life. I don't want that to happen to me, and I recognize a very profound loneliness in myself.
>
> I have my deep experiences alone, then I tell my friends. I don't have deep meaningful experiences with them. So that's another safety valve I have. I think this involves my lack of trust. My father told me, "Nobody likes you. They only pretend to like you." That was his own projection. I think it really did affect me. I'm always waiting for somebody to pull out on me.

As in Ray's experience, our relationships with others can be affected unconsciously by our parents' comments, projections, and unspoken judgments. After the death of a loved one, when our new clarity allows us to see so much of ourselves anew, we may begin to recognize such projections and challenge their power over us.

To summarize, then, the death of a loved one within the family can make or break a friendship. Note how Robin, Ray, and Gloria began to take their friendships more seriously. All three accepted responsibility for deepening potentially enriching friendships while dropping those they came to identify as draining and unfulfilling. These three join many others in realizing that the experience of losing a loved one has made them better friends with an increased capacity for compassion, honesty, and understanding.

Communicating with Friends

Since communication with friends can be difficult or strained while you are grieving, it is helpful to have several communication options. If it becomes difficult to talk to your friend, try writing a letter. If that doesn't work for you, internal communication techniques can help you deal with sensitive issues, express your feelings, and gain an understanding of the other person's position. For example, you might want to use your imagination to meet your friend in a healing place or to carry on an internal dialogue.

- Let your friends know what you want and need from them. Offer them some suggestions of ways they can help and support you—perhaps by bringing you a meal, doing some errands, giving you a backrub, taking a walk with you, or checking in on you regularly. Make it clear that you need to withdraw (*if* you do). Encourage your friends to educate themselves about grief so that they will know what to expect. Remind them that grief takes a long time to heal.
- If you feel too vulnerable or overwhelmed to have a conversation, write your friend a letter, stating what you need and want as well as what your friendship means to you. Identify anything the friend is doing that runs counter to your needs. For example, your friend may be avoiding talking about your grief, even though you want to.
- If you don't want to communicate but need to work on some unresolved issues in the relationship, use internal communication techniques, particularly exercise 7-1, "An Internal Encounter with a Living Family Member," in chapter 7.
- When you feel ready, talk with your friend. Refer to exercise 7-2, "An External Encounter," in chapter 7. Prepare carefully by thinking through your concerns ahead of time so you can identify and address any changes that may have occurred in your friendship as a result of your grieving.

How You Can Support a Grieving Friend

To better support your grieving friend, remember that using internal communication techniques will help you maintain a connection with your friend even if he or she has withdrawn from you. You can work with imagery to meet your friend in an imaginal world, write a letter, or create a dialogue. These suggestions will also help you integrate grief into your friendship day to day:

- Educate yourself about what your grieving friend is going through. Read books on grief, listen to tapes, talk with others who have grieved. You can expect your grieving friend to be emotional, raw, restless, and unpredictable. Don't expect normalcy too soon. Your friend may want to be with you sometimes and alone at others. He or she may want to talk sometimes and remain silent with you at others. Take your friend's lead.
- It is important to acknowledge the death and the impact it has had on your friend. Recognize that your friend is in an altered state. Understand if you can that moods will shift abruptly and that simple contact can be greatly soothing. Express interest in your friend's feelings and concerns. Remember that you don't have to make your friend feel better. If your friend cries, be as supportive as you can. If your friend needs to talk, listen. Be trustworthy with confidences. Avoid giving lots of advice, even though you may feel impelled to do this because you feel helpless in the face of so much pain.
- Help in small ways. You can bring meals and flowers, offer to do errands, send cards, and check in regularly by phone.
- Be willing to admit your helplessness in the situation and be honest if you feel overwhelmed or frightened by the intensity of your friend's feelings. You may need to pull back for a while. If so, let your friend know that you are doing this.

- Try not to take rejection personally. Many people who are grieving don't have the energy to be considerate or nice.
- Your friendship will probably change throughout your friend's grief. Some friendships deepen, but some drift away. Grieve the loss of the old friendship and be open to changes.

A friendship is deeply affected, even transformed, by grief. Those who have lost a loved one often feel committed to enhancing the quality of their friendships, which can lead to a deepening of some relationships and termination of others. Those who are grieving may demand more of their friends but find, too, that once the most consuming stage of grief is passed, they are able to give more, particularly when called to support friends through a similar life transition.

From the point of view of the friend, while some people may feel catalyzed to support a friend in grief, others may feel overwhelmed by the intensity of that grief and pull away. Thomas Moore reminds us that in either case the friendship may live on in the imagination: "Eternity makes itself felt in both lasting relationships and those that last only a short time. In neither case is the soul concerned with literal time, but rather with the tone of the event. If it evokes eternity, then the friendship itself remains in imagination for endless time, even if the personal relationship does not" (Moore, p. 97).

In confronting our aloneness and mortality when we lose a loved one, we renew contact with ourselves, discover who we are, and risk a new definition of ourselves. With a clearer sense of self and the willingness to communicate while respecting differences, we can define with new clarity our position in a relationship, one that is based on our own priorities and values. This new congruence of inner and outer realities can enable us to act rather than merely react, thus building the basis for real communication and intimacy in our relationships.

11

Healing Grief Passed Down through Generations

In our own imaginations, we construct bridges to history, to cultures
far from ours in time and tone. We recognize and join, even if only
in the imagination, the hidden communities of the human family,
wherever they may be in time or eternity.
Ann and Barry Ulanov

As I was growing up, we never talked about death in my family. It wasn't until I was a mother myself that I realized the impact this was having on my life. My six-year-old son was just beginning to be curious about death and was asking questions about it. When he asked my father, "Are you going to die, Granddad?" my father dismissed him with a gruff, "Of course not." The subject was closed. It hit me in that moment that my father was passing along his denial of death to my son. A year later my father was dying of cancer—and he still didn't talk about his illness or his dying.

I began to understand how deeply my father had been wounded by his mother's unresolved grief. She had lost her youngest son in World War II, and her loss consumed the rest of her life and contaminated all those around her. She grieved continuously, going over and over her memories of her now-idealized relationship with her son. She was mired in her grief, unable to let go and move on with the rest of her life. My father, who returned from the war unharmed, was ignored. He had come back with his own grief over the friends he had lost and the horror he had witnessed, but he had no support or encouragement to talk about it. He also suffered from being invisible to his mother. He buried this grief deep inside, the only signs of it erupting in nightmares that haunted his sleep for many years.

When I was sixteen I visited my grandparents' home in New Jersey. I thought it strange that the old-fashioned living room of this old farmhouse was filled with pictures of their dead son. There was not one of my father. My grandmother's unresolved grief and consequent inability to give love and attention to the living eroded my father's already shaky sense of self-worth. He was unable to talk about death or grief and hence could not even answer honestly the innocent question of his six-year-old grandchild.

In the months leading up to my father's death, my son and I had many talks at bedtime regarding his concerns about death. My son realized that if my father was dying, it meant that I too could die. Some of his questions were hard for me to face—for example, "What will happen to me when you die? Who will take care of me? Can't I die before you?" His tears pulled at my heart. But in acknowledging his fears, exploring his questions, and embracing the mystery of death along with my son, I could see a deeper appreciation for the preciousness of life developing within him. And I saw subtle signs that he was beginning to accept death as a natural part of the life cycle.

I didn't just grieve my father when he died. I opened to the grief that had been suppressed by my father and to the grief that had consumed my grandmother. I understood that embracing my grief fully was a healing of three generations. If I hadn't learned how to grieve, my grandmother's and my father's unresolved grief could easily have been passed down through me to my son. And ironically, just as my father had been silent about death and grief, speaking about grief has become an integral part of my work and daily life. I've had to speak up for all the silent generations, for all of us who have been wounded by the silence we've experienced around death and grief.

I have become convinced that some people can unknowingly carry the unresolved grief of past generations. Most often they are not aware of

this until we begin to explore their family history. When I hear that someone has lost a child, sibling, or parent and never grieved that loss, I am
alerted to the possibility that this person could be carrying the grief of a
parent—or grandparent or great-grandparent.

Marcie consulted me months after a miscarriage. She could not
understand why she had not recovered emotionally in all this time. Her
depression had deepened, which frightened her. Exploring several disturbing dreams about her mother, she shared with me that her mother
had lost her five-year-old daughter in an auto accident months before
Marcie was conceived. Her mother was depressed throughout her preg-
nancy but felt convinced that this little baby would make her life worth
living again. She tried to focus on the baby growing inside her and did not
grieve the loss of her child.

Marcie most likely absorbed her mother's unresolved grief when
she was in the womb. Babies and children are particularly vulnerable to
absorbing the inner conflicts of their parents, as Frances Wickes so elo-
quently argues in her classic book *The Inner World of Childhood*: "I have
known many cases where children were forced to bear the sins of their
ancestors, not because of inheritance but because ghosts were fastened
to them by the process of projection and identification" (Wickes, p. 34).
Throughout her childhood Marcie was very bonded to her mother and
responded readily to her mother's needs. Wickes states that it is the
most-loved child who can suffer most from a parent's unresolved conflicts because the child's unconscious is brought into a close relationship with that of her parents. This was certainly true for Marcie, who was
an only child.

When Marcie was fifteen, her father died, leaving Marcie's mother
incapacitated by grief. The accumulated grief of her child's and husband's
deaths had broken through her coping mechanisms. Marcie's mother
talked incessantly about her dead husband and daughter and seemed
unable to focus on her family's needs. Marcie valiantly struggled to hold

the family together, even after she married, until her own grief over her miscarriage plunged her into depression. During our work together, Marcie had to extricate her own grief from her mother's. She also found that she had to separate herself emotionally from her mother. She learned how to protect herself from her mother's feelings, how to identify her own feelings, how to grieve her losses (she had never had the support to grieve her father's death), and how to set boundaries with her family of origin so that she could focus on her relationship with her own husband and children.

As is true for many people who carry the unresolved grief of generations, once Marcie uncovered the grief she had carried unknowingly through her childhood, many aspects of her life suddenly made sense. Friends and family members had consistently commented on how serious and sensitive Marcie had been as a child. Marcie had always felt responsible for her mother's happiness but never knew why. Her mother had expected her to fill the hole left by a dead child, a task Marcie of course could never fulfill. This new awareness was an immense relief for Marcie, and realizing that her mother's grief was not hers, she now turned to grieve her own loss with deep commitment. And as is often reported by clients at this stage of healing, she experienced a new lightness of being.

A Nightmare Opens the Door to Healing
Three Generations of Unresolved Grief

Another person who worked with me discovered through a series of nightmares that he was the third generation to carry his grandmother's unresolved grief from the Holocaust. Josh grew alarmed when he began awakening each night at 2 A.M. from the same nightmare. In the dream, as a boy about seven years old, he was running across a square in a European village when a Nazi soldier shot him. The boy fell to the ground and then watched in horror as the soldier stepped closer and kicked him hard with his boot. At this point, sweating profusely and moaning, Josh always awakened from the dream. He had had occasional nightmares before, but never like this. The same frightening dream repeated over and over. And the imagery disturbed him, the dream being so violent and disconnected from anything in his daily life. After two weeks the dreams showed no signs of leaving. Exhausted, he asked his wife, who was my client, for my telephone number. She was grieving the death of her father, using her sanctuary daily, and experiencing a healing in her relationship with her father. It is likely that sharing in his wife's grief activated the grief that was buried in Josh's psyche. Knowing that he now had access to a structured and safe way to grieve, his unconscious may have taken an opportunity to heal.

In my office, Josh and I explored the images of his dream, along with the dramatic effect it was having on him. This dream was clearly not going to let him alone until he worked with it. It seemed to me that something very powerful was lurking under the surface, ready to come to consciousness. I knew that the dreams would give us feedback as we worked. If we were off-base, the dream would continue as it was. If we made progress, the dream would change and show us where we needed to explore next. The dream puzzled Josh because it was so removed from his own experiences. Why would he be dreaming about a little boy killed by the Nazis?

Asking him for any associations with European villages and Nazis, I learned that his grandparents were Orthodox Jews living in a small European village during World War II. While his rabbi grandfather was visiting the United States on a business trip, Nazi soldiers broke into his grandparents' home, raping his grandmother in front of the children (one of whom was Josh's father) and savagely cutting her face. The grandfather returned and brought the devastated family back to the United States. His grandmother never spoke again and withdrew from all family interaction. His grandfather did his best to hold the family together as the Holocaust went on, killing most family members who had remained in Europe. For many years the trauma was never discussed in the family, although the unresolved grief took its toll. Josh's grandmother remained withdrawn and silent until her death. Josh's father grew up to be angry and abusive; Josh left home early, full of anger and bitterness.

As he shared his family history, it became clear to Josh how much unresolved grief his family carried and how this grief had been passed down from generation to generation. It seemed that he had unconsciously touched upon a deep collective image within his family system, and now this image was demanding some response. We decided to start with his grandmother, for her unresolved grief seemed pivotal and her silence had impacted several generations of her family. I asked Josh to set aside time each day to just be with his grandmother in his imagination—to open to her pain, to listen if she wanted to speak.

Driving home from that first session, he clearly heard his grandmother saying "My dear one" in Yiddish to him. He had never heard her speak before, but he knew that it was her voice. Pulling his car to the side of the road, he wept. Each day after that he closed his eyes and sat with his grandmother on the back porch of their old home on the East Coast. For days they just sat side by side in silence, looking out over two large sugar maple trees. Then his grandmother began to talk to him, sharing with him her pain, regrets, and sorrow. And as she did this, he started to feel lighter himself. His heart opened to his grandmother as she softened in her vulnerability.

Josh's nightmares did not return after that first session, so we had feedback that his unconscious was satisfied with the work he was doing on healing his family trauma. Josh felt extraordinary changes in himself as well—he yearned to connect with Judaism for the first time and began to study the Torah. Becoming intimately aware of the pain that his father had experienced in his childhood, he felt a strange sense of forgiveness for a man he had despised. He told me that he wanted to come to peace with his father but wasn't ready yet to talk to him.

After six weeks, Josh had the dream again. This time the little boy was again shot by the Nazi soldier, but as the soldier moved in to deliver the devastating kick, the child's family surrounded the boy, lifting him up and cradling him protectively. Josh awakened, crying this time not from fear and anguish but from a sense of joy and belonging. It was clear from this dream that Josh had healed something deep within himself. He had also brought healing to the family psyche that had carried such deep grief.

Look for signs of buried or unresolved grief in your family. Investigate thoroughly your family history. Did your parents, grandparents, or great-grandparents experience any major losses? How did they respond to those losses? Was death or grief discussed openly? Were there taboos around these subjects? Be on the alert for nightmares that may point to a buried family grief, as Josh's nightmares did.

If you do uncover grief that has been passed down through generations, set aside time each day in your sanctuary. Place a picture on your altar of the family member who experienced the loss. Experiment with the exercises in part two. You can talk to your family member or write a letter or dialogue. You can explore guided imagery, as Josh did as he sat in his imagination every day for several weeks with his grandmother on her back porch. In this process, open your heart to your family member's pain. Encourage this person to express and heal their grief. But at the same time, it is critically important that you maintain clarity that this grief belongs to them, not to you.

Exercise 11-1
HEALING THE GRIEF PASSED DOWN THROUGH GENERATIONS

Sit down, close your eyes, and focus your awareness on your breathing, breathing into your belly. Relaxing tensions as you exhale, become more and more present to this moment. Notice the feelings and sensations that are occurring now.

Feel your awareness expanding, transcending the limitations of space and time. Your imagination is fluid here, full of possibilities for healing.

Imagine yourself in a peaceful place where you can nourish your spirit—in the mountains, in a forest, by the sea. Create the scenery around you, experiencing its sounds, sights, and smells. Let there be a body of water nearby—perhaps a river, lake, or the ocean. Take some time to relax in this place, absorbing the tranquillity and peace.

Invite your family member to join you here for the purpose of healing the unresolved grief that has been passed down through the generations. Introduce him/her to this place, again taking time to take in the peacefulness so that both of you are relaxed and receptive. There is no need to hurry.

Find a comfortable place to sit with your family member. Now invite him/her to share with you the grief that has been held in his heart. You are simply to listen as he gives expression to feelings that may have never been expressed. As you listen, you are able to see with the eyes of the imagination the unresolved grief in his heart. What does it look like? What color is it? What texture? Look into your own heart. Do you see that same unresolved grief hidden there?

When your family member has finished sharing, ask if he or she is ready to let that grief go now. If he is not, let him know that you will be returning on another day to talk and be together for further healing.

If your family member is ready to let go of that grief, invite her to gather that grief, scooping it out of her heart with her hands. Walk with her as she carries that grief to the river, sea, or lake where she will throw it into the water. Watch as that grief dissolves and disappears; it is being cleansed and transformed.

If that unresolved grief has been passed down to you, gently gather it from your heart into your hands—this grief does not belong to you. Carry it to the water and place it in the water where it can be cleansed and transformed. Again, watch it dissolve and disappear. Experience what it feels like to no longer be carrying this grief.

After this is done, just be together with your family member. Feel the peace that is within you—know that peace is within you.

The Patterns That Get Passed Down from
Generation to Generation

The time of a parent's or grandparent's death can be a fertile time for gathering and assessing information about your family history from your surviving parent and other relatives. In doing this, you may become aware of certain themes or patterns that thread through the generations. Do you see patterns in your parents' relationship that are similar to those in your own marriage or intimate relationship? Did your grandparents or great-grandparents struggle with the same issues you face now? Do you want to continue these patterns in your own life?

Family patterns get passed down until one family member stops to ask, "Is this actually appropriate or healthy for me? Is this what I really want in my life or my relationships?"

Use internal communication to explore patterns and conditioning that have affected each generation. Write a letter to a deceased family member, expressing your concern about issues that he or she had strug- gled with and that you find yourself facing today. You can also write your family member's response.

Shirley saw a disturbing pattern of sexual oppression affecting the women of her maternal lineage. As a mother of two daughters, she felt compelled to break the cycle. In a letter, she turned to her grandmother— who had died years before—for guidance, advice, and support. Her grandmother's love had sustained her through her childhood, and she felt it would now help her face a shameful family issue.

Dear Grandma,

As I start this letter, tears well up in my eyes and my chest muscles tighten. I miss you so much. You were so soft and kind in a world of pain and confusion. When it felt like my whole family was against me, you lovingly took me into your arms. You alone saw me as special.

Being in your presence was like a gift from God. I felt safe and loved. I have to admit though, Grandma, I didn't like Grandpa too much. He scared me. He seemed mean and ornery and always held on to us too long and too tight when he hugged us. I feel ashamed to admit this, but I felt kind of glad when he died. It's funny, nobody else seemed too heartbroken either. I don't remember my mother crying.

I loved the big green and white house you lived in. It was always a mystery to me. I often wondered what went on inside this three-story house with seven children. What did you think of Grandpa as a husband/father? I wish you could tell me some stories about my mother.

The upstairs is where my mother's bedroom was. She did not seem to like visiting her old room, nor did I. How come? What happened? Mom says she has some vague memories of being sexually molested by Grandpa. Were you ever molested? How come your mother, who lived right across the street, wouldn't talk to you? I heard she didn't like Grandpa. Is that true? How come she didn't like Grandpa?

After Grandpa died, your energy became lighter. Even so, there was a sadness in your chocolate-brown eyes, a sadness that spoke of eons of oppression. I know it sounds weird, but I feel like you and my entire maternal ancestry are counting on me to end the oppression. This is so hard. When you died I felt so all alone, like a safety net had been pulled out from underneath me. I was only fourteen years old and a victim of oppression myself.

Grandma, I just want you to know that I am fighting back. I will change the history of our lineage. I have two daughters of my own now, and it is up to me to break the cycle. I will not allow the oppression to continue one generation longer. Your sadness is my strength. I know you are with me, guiding me, cheering me on, and loving me.

About a year ago I felt your presence so strongly that I felt moved to erect a shrine in your memory. Since your death I have undergone many changes. I married at age twenty and had two daughters shortly thereafter. Unlike everyone else in the family, I've managed to go to college and am currently working on my master's degree. Difficult as it was and will continue to be, I have gained a sense of freedom from the oppression that has plagued the women of this family for centuries. I hope you can feel it too. I can now accept your death as part of the ongoing cycle of life, and although I miss you very much, I know that things are as they should be.

With love and gratitude,

Shirley

Connecting with her grandmother through this letter helped Shirley access her own inner strength. She felt resolved to be the instrument of change in her family system: "I will not allow the oppression to continue one generation longer. Your sadness is my strength. I know you are with me, guiding me, cheering me on, and loving me."

Becoming aware of challenging family patterns can be painful, but such pain can be a powerful motivation to change. When we set about creating change, there can be strong resistance not only from within the family but also from within the self. It can feel terrifying and lonely to break out of a pattern that is deeply entrenched in the family history. However, the death of a loved one can provide just the momentum needed to break through this inevitable resistance.

Like Shirley, I was an instrument of change in my family. It was frightening but liberating to break the silence around my father's cancer and then to write about his death. The healing radiated out to my family. My mother and I freely talked about her mortality and my fears about her dying. I wrote her a letter in which I shared with her everything I would want to tell her after she died.

When my son was ten, an exchange happened between us that could never have taken place with my father or between my grandmother and her son. After a book-signing party for *Losing a Parent*, my son and I were walking toward our car in the parking lot. Suddenly he threw his arms around me and told me with great confidence and enthusiasm, "Mama, you'll be so proud of me. When you die, I'll write *Losing a Parent Part II!*" I was a bit taken aback but pleasantly surprised. As a family we were able to talk about and explore this great mystery of death. The taboo of past generations had been broken.

12

Healing Daily Losses

The Way is gained by daily loss.
Chuang Tzu

I was feeling a heavy heart as I returned home from my son's college cam-
pus, where I helped him move into his apartment for his second year.
I know the time is coming when he will not return home from college for
the summer. Last year when we left him, I cried all the way back from Los
Angeles. I sobbed for the ending of my relationship with my son as it had
been, of our family as it had been, for the absence of his daily presence in
my life.

At midlife, I've lost my father and face the loss of my mother, who at
eighty-six grows increasingly frail and forgetful. She's been falling lately.
The last fall left her hospitalized for weeks. In addition, four of my
friends are struggling with life-threatening illnesses, once again forcing
me to let go of the persistent illusion that we can control our lives. In an
instant the course of our lives can change. This is terrifying. I feel vulnerable and at times frightened by the magnitude of daily loss at this
stage of life. Ironically, I have never felt more alive.

Over a lifetime we will experience many losses. We live by losing,
leaving, and letting go. These are essential parts of the ever-changing
world, as much a part of life as night, wind, and rain. We cannot save ourselves, nor those we love, from the sorrow that is part of life. Parents die,
friends drop away, cherished possessions are lost. Our children grow up
and leave home. We lose spouses and partners to divorce or death; sometimes we lose them emotionally long before. As we age, we will confront

all that we never were or never will be. We will be faced with the grief of unfulfilled dreams. With each major loss, we often encounter multiple losses. For example, the death of a parent can lead to many other losses—of our identity as their child, of our family history, and sometimes of friends as they retreat from the intensity of our grief. Losing a job can lead to the loss of self-confidence, identity, and power. A miscarriage or infertility can bring about the loss of the dream of having a family. A divorce can result in the loss of a lifestyle, home, friends, and identity.

Living as we do in a culture that is based on acquisition, most of us naturally shrink from loss. We are tempted to think that we can avoid the pain of loss if we keep busy, that we can close our hearts a little to protect ourselves. However, it is the ungrieved losses that take their toll on our hearts and deaden us. We forget that even these, as difficult as they may be, are connected to our vitality and growth. Irish poet John O'Donohue calls loss the "sister of discovery." He explains that as it empties and clears away the old, loss makes room for something new. It allows us to grow and enjoy new things. Loss provides a "vital clearance of the soul." It prunes away the dead branches so that new shoots can break forth.

Many people don't recognize this deep undercurrent of loss until they lose a loved one. It wasn't until Bonnie lost her mother that she began to acknowledge how much loss was weighing on her heart. In her first session, Bonnie shared that her accumulated losses over the past ten years felt like quicksand, pulling her into a deep depression. She listed for me loss after loss—of freedom when she became a mother, of friends and community when she moved, of her health after three pregnancies, of intimacy with her husband as they both juggled hectic schedules, of contact with her siblings, financial losses, the death of her father and, most recently, of her mother. Her life had swept her along while the losses accumulated—unfelt, unacknowledged, unresolved. Now it was the profound grief over her mother which made her realize that grief had always been there, just under the surface. Bonnie realized how all that accumulated ordinary grief had shut her down and compromised her aliveness. And she found that she was now weeping for her greatest loss of all—the many unlived moments of her life.

If we could recognize this ordinary grief sooner, we wouldn't feel so overwhelmed when a loved one dies. When we open to the little losses, we make room in our hearts for the greater losses. We gain strength to grieve when a major loss shakes our world. If we pay attention even to small losses, we will find that they tap into that reservoir of loss we hold inside. If we but, in the words of poet David Whyte, "slip beneath the still surface of the well of grief," we will find the "source from which we drink."

Creating a Loss Timeline

Take some time now to reflect on the losses of your life. Draw a timeline, your birth at the far left end, the present moment at the right end. Along this line mark the losses you've experienced and write the loss above it. Include major losses as well as ordinary ones. Then circle the losses that are still unresolved and ungrieved. When a loss activates an earlier one, draw an arrow from that loss to the earlier one.

Once you finish this part of the process, reflect on your timeline. Take in the full spectrum of loss that you have experienced in your lifetime; indeed, many people doing this timeline are struck with the amount of loss they have experienced: "I didn't realize how many losses I had experienced, how many losses I never grieved." Take time to look at the patterns of these losses. You may notice that there are clusters of losses, losses that brought about other losses or circled back to earlier losses. Reflect on what effect these unresolved losses have had on your life.

Many of us resist grieving because we are afraid of feeling overwhelmed, of becoming nonfunctional: "If I start crying, I'll never stop." We tell ourselves that time will heal. However, the unresolved losses remain buried in our hearts and in our bodies. We end up shutting down on life because we feel we can't afford to be near anything that might trigger our grief. Many of my clients have current problems that are rooted in a past loss which was never grieved. Unresolved grief can lead to such symptoms as depression, social isolation, addictions, and chronic physical symptoms. It is much healthier to take a proactive approach to grieving our daily losses, to embrace our grief in small doses, to heal our losses one by one. Then we realize that no part of our life's journey is wasted; there is a gift in every loss.

Now that you have identified these losses on your timeline, make a commitment to use your sanctuary for several days or weeks for the purpose of healing these losses. During this time, open your heart to your grief, for it is in the heart that the healing takes place.

Exercise 12-1
OPENING THE HEART

Close your eyes and focus on the heart center at your sternum between your breasts, that same point which you focused on in exercise 2-2, "Connecting through Your Heart with a Dying Loved One," in chapter 2. You may want to use your thumb to press gently into that point. Breathe into this point as you push into the sensitivity there. Each breath carries you deeper into your heart. Slowly open to the pain held there, the losses of a lifetime hidden away in the dark corners.

Let your heart experience all the pain of loss—the loss of your parents, of your children, of your dreams, the separation from those you love, the grief of putting yourself out of your own heart. Let your heart open to these losses. Cradle them with compassion. Feel the grief, the ache, the longing—all the tears unshed, the moments unlived. Make room in your heart for the pain and for the healing. Keep breathing into your heart, feeling it grow more spacious. Learn to not close your heart when there is pain.

Healing Our Unresolved Losses

Bringing so many losses to the surface can feel at first overwhelming. But as I recommend to clients facing several deaths at once, you can focus on one loss at a time after each session of heart opening. You may want to focus on the most recent loss, or the one that has the greatest emotional charge. Your dreams may guide you to the loss that most needs your attention, as Alice's story below will demonstrate. Place a picture or object that reminds you of this loss on the altar of your sanctuary. Spend a period of time there each day, opening to whatever feelings you have avoided, ignored, or tried to avoid around this loss. Don't analyze; just embrace the feelings as they are.

Alice discovered that her unresolved grief over the loss of her marriage had closed her heart and kept her from being able to grieve her mother's death. She had been struggling with her grief and felt frustrated that she couldn't let down and cry. Early in our work together I guided her through an "Opening the Heart" exercise. It surprised her how many unresolved losses were stashed away in her heart. The space within felt dark and crowded, so crowded that it was almost impossible to access her grief for her mother. In her third session, she shared a dream in which her ex-husband knocked at her door, asking for her help with his car. He wanted to fix the car so that they could take a small trip together. She awakened feeling annoyed and perplexed that her ex-husband had showed up in her dream. Not wanting to focus on him at all in the therapy, she eagerly changed the focus of our session back to her father. However, the next week she shared two more dreams about her ex-husband, at which point I gently encouraged her to follow the lead of her unconscious. Her heart had opened in her grief, and this was the unresolved issue that was asking for her attention.

Alice begrudgingly agreed to talk about her marriage, the end of which had been very painful for her. While she was caring for her dying mother, her husband had had an affair. When Alice found out, she was devastated by the betrayal at such a vulnerable time and immediately asked for a divorce. She now deeply resented that the precious last few months with her dying mother had passed without her being able to be fully present since she had been consumed with anger, hurt, and resentment toward her husband.

Alice resisted my suggestion to write a letter to her husband, one that she wouldn't send (see chapter 4). She didn't want to open to these excruciating feelings again. It took four weeks to begin the letter, but once she started writing she found it difficult to stop. She wrote pages and still didn't feel finished. The next week she wrote more. She began to feel lighter and more at peace with this painful part of her history. As she was completing the letter, she had a long-awaited dream about her mother. It was time now to grieve her beloved parent's death; the divorce no longer stood in the way.

That week she also had another dream about her ex-husband. In this resolution dream, his family had gathered for a festive party in his mother's backyard. Alice was delighted to see the family again, many of whom she had cared deeply for but had lost contact with after her divorce. She connected with each one, hugging her mother-in-law a long time. Through opening to the pain of her divorce, she could also now open to the riches this marriage had given her. Even with some lurking anger for her husband, she finally felt at peace with him. With this healing, her focus in therapy turned to grieving the loss of her mother, which she could now do with her whole heart.

Like so many people, Alice had avoided grieving the end of her marriage. Not only was this excruciatingly painful, but she just didn't give this loss the weight that she did the death of her mother. However, with the closing of her heart to this pain, she had also closed her heart to the grief over her mother's death. During the years that followed she had felt devastated that she couldn't even cry. In seeking help for her predicament, she soon discovered that her own dreams were guiding her back to the unresolved feelings from her divorce. Clearly, Alice's story teaches us that sometimes we must attend to the other losses we haven't grieved—whether a marriage, friendship, job, or lifelong dream—before we can open to the really big ones.

Periodically, take time to review your daily losses, and then grieve them. Pay attention when a current loss brings up one from the past that is unresolved. Grieve that loss as well. Experiencing this grief will keep your heart spacious and open to life. Loss by loss, we will follow the trail back to ourselves. There we find, as Bonnie did, the greatest loss—our grief for ourselves: for all the unlived moments, for the times we have not been true to ourselves, for the ways we have compromised ourselves, for what we have sacrificed to win the approval of others or to be successful.

I was deeply moved when a client, who was grieving both her parents' deaths, shared with me that she had recently set her parents' pictures to one side of her altar and placed a picture of herself at the center—a photograph of herself at four years old, arms stretched out in welcome to the photographer, a smile just as wide across as her face, and eyes lit up with wonder and excitement for life. After months of grieving the loss of her parents, she was now grieving herself, the loss of that openness to life. In opening to that grief, she couldn't bear to hold back from life any longer. She knew she could now bear the exquisite beauty and the sorrow of being fully alive. Each moment was becoming precious, an opportunity to embrace the wonder of life—the separations, meetings, conflicts, peace, and, yes, all the losses.

Epilogue

*May you know that absence is full of tender presence and that nothing
is ever lost or forgotten. May the sore well of grief turn into a
well of seamless presence.*
John O'Donohue

"The end is where we start from," writes T. S. Eliot. When we come to the final pages of a book, we have reached an ending, but if that book has been meaningful to us, the end of a book is also a beginning. As we close the cover, we take within ourselves what has touched and inspired us. Whatever we have read on the page can then become a part of us and of our lives. So it is when a loved one dies. That life is over. Yet if that person has touched you deeply, he or she becomes a part of you. You will carry that person within yourself always. Many other cultures took this process for granted; nurturing the relationships with the ancestors is an integral part of the fabric of daily life. Deep down, we know this too—but we have to be reminded.

I hope this book has challenged any assumptions that have made it difficult for you to connect with a deceased loved one—for example, that death has severed your relationships with loved ones, that it is too late to reconcile, and that you must resign yourself to living with your memories and regrets. I encourage you to let your imagination lead you past these limiting concepts into the unknown, where possibilities beyond your wildest dreams await you. Your imagination is a creative entity, an animating and healing force that can restore to you those you had considered lost.

Imagination heals by stretching you—beyond your comfort zone—into new experiences. Until her imagination gave her this experience,

Kira couldn't conceive of tenderly rocking her father. Until her imagination allowed her to see, Candace considered it impossible to witness her father's life through his eyes. Many of the vignettes Candace witnessed were painful for her to face, particularly that scene in which her father tried unsuccessfully to leave a marriage that was controlled by his mother-in-law. Imagination heals if you can wait for what comes and risk seeing and hearing what it sets before you.

As you commit to cultivating and deepening your relationships with deceased loved ones—or with those who are living, for that matter—the internal communication exercises in this book will enable you to express love, work through unresolved issues, and find new possibilities for relating. Take advantage of the freedoms that the imagination provides: to express yourself without restriction, to break out of old patterns of relating, to step inside another person. You may feel exhilarated and excited as you make breakthroughs in old relationship impasses. You may feel immensely grateful to receive or give love that had not been possible when the person was alive. You may also feel vulnerable and raw as you touch old wounds or break through old taboos. And sometimes, to be sure, you may feel discouraged and resistant as you face unpleasant realizations or uncomfortable feelings.

You will experience many of these feelings and pass through several stages as you build a new relationship. First, you must experience the freedom of expressing what you think, feel, and want, including whatever has been repressed, held back, or silenced in your relationship. Amy vented her regrets and resentments in her letter to her deceased father; only then did she feel ready to forgive herself and him. Expressing yourself honestly and authentically to another person in the imagination will help build a sense of self-worth and confidence that is essential in building a healthy relationship.

In the second stage of building a new relationship through writing or speaking a response, you learn to provide a voice to the other person. As you do this, you may feel yourself to be simultaneously within yourself and within the other person, an experience that puts you in touch with that person's feelings and thoughts. This can be even more dramatic when, working with imagery, you step inside another and see the world through his or her eyes. Suddenly you understand the relationship from the other person's perspective. Compassion, understanding, and even forgiveness develop naturally at this stage.

In the third stage, a new relationship has finally emerged. Be prepared for changes in your relationship that didn't seem possible before. As you communicate with your loved one, the dialogue shifts from resolving past issues to an expression of intimacy in the present. After repeated experiences of connecting with your beloved through the imagination, your heart will acknowledge a comforting, affirming presence abiding within—a presence you now trust to be accessible whenever summoned.

But you'll find that this presence incorporates more than you thought—a sense of luminosity, wisdom, and immeasurable peace. You have come face-to-face with a sacred life force that pulses at the center of every being. Through cultivating and deepening your inner relationship with your loved one, you will have touched the divine.

Suggestions for Grieving
and
Exercises for Healing
Relationships beyond Loss

Ten Steps to Grieving the Loss of a Loved One

1. *Acknowledge the importance and power of this event.* The death of a loved one shakes the very foundation of our lives. It is natural, though often uncomfortable, to feel raw and vulnerable, alone, out of control. Rather than resisting the powerful forces activated in grief, learn strategies for moving through it, stage by stage, day by day.

2. *Take time each day to honor your grief.* Set up a sanctuary in your home or in nature, a protected place where you can open fully to your grief for ten to twenty minutes every day. Using the sanctuary, gradually you will find a rhythm of entering the grief for a period each day and then letting it go and attending to daily tasks.

3. *Address any unfinished business with your loved one.* It is common for unresolved feelings toward your loved one to surface after his or her death. The grieving period is an important time to heal these old wounds and begin to say good-bye.

4. *Participate in creating new family patterns.* The family system is often thrown into chaos and upheaval after a parent's death. Old patterns don't work with the same predictable results. The family may thrash around for months, seeking a new balance with one another. This is a brief window of opportunity when the family is opened up to change before a new system is established. You can either be thrown into this new system or consciously participate in creating new patterns that are healthy for you.

5. *Explore the direction and quality of your life.* The death of a loved one often initiates a period of painful questioning: Where am I going in my life? What do I really value? What are my beliefs? Does my life really matter? This questioning is a critical part of the grieving process. Out of it will come new perspectives, directions, and choices.

6. *Don't pressure yourself to "get back to normal."* Many expect that grief will be over in a few weeks or months. Grief has its own rhythm, nature, and timing that resist our attempts to control it. For some, though certainly not all, there is a marked shift around the first anniversary of your parent's death. However, as the years pass, the grief may well up from time to time. Each time it surfaces, see it as an opportunity for more healing.

7. *Give yourself nurturance, love, protection, and encouragement.* Clarify the expectations you had of your loved one that he or she never could fulfill. In seeing the relationship for what it was rather than what you wanted it to be, you can grieve what your loved one didn't give you and begin to appreciate what he or she did give you.

8. *Let your friends know what you want and need from them.* Offer them some suggestions of ways that they can help and support you—perhaps bringing you a meal, doing some errands, giving you a backrub, taking a walk with you, checking in on you regularly. Assert your need to withdraw. Let him or her know about anything that he or she is doing that is not supportive. Encourage your friends to educate themselves about grief so that they will know what to expect. Remind them that grief takes a long time to heal.

9. *Each year acknowledge the anniversary of your loved one's death.* Take time to reflect and do something special to commemorate that date. Be gentle with yourself, as this is a vulnerable time in which many may feel depressed or emotional.

10. *Celebrate the changes and new perspectives.* These will begin to manifest in your life as you move out of the dark middle phase of grief. When you feel ready, act on new ideas, inspirations, and insights.

Seven Tasks of Grieving

It's important to actively work to integrate and resolve our grief, not to just passively experience our reactions to it. *Grief carries us until we learn to carry it*. There are tasks in grieving, and the sanctuary is a good place to work on them. These tasks are to

1. Express all the feelings over the loss: anguish, longing, relief, anger, depression, numbness, despair, aching, guilt, confusion, and often unbearable pain.
2. Let the nonnegotiable and excruciating reality sink in that you will never again be in the physical presence of your deceased loved one.
3. Review your relationship from the beginning and see the positive and negative aspects of the person and the relationship.
4. Identify and heal your unresolved issues and your regrets.
5. Explore the changes in your family and other relationships.
6. Integrate all the changes into a new sense of yourself and take on healthy new ways of being in the world without this person.
7. Form a healthy new inner relationship with this person and find new ways of relating to him or her.

Sanctuary Exercise

Sit quietly in your sanctuary, bringing your full attention to your grief. Take a few minutes to reflect on your loved one who is dying or has died, acknowledging this loss. Feel where the grief is residing in your body right now. Note how it surfaces in your thoughts and feelings. Grief changes from month to month, from week to week, from day to day, even from moment to moment. Give it your full attention. Don't assume that what you felt yesterday is what you are feeling today.

Be present with your grief as it is right now without judging, without criticizing, without trying to change anything. If feelings surface, let them flow. Trust them as they present themselves. Don't push them back, don't push them away. It's safe here in your sanctuary. If you are feeling numb, you may at first feel that nothing is going on, but if you look closer you may discover that even numbness involves a complicated set of sensations and experiences. So don't judge yourself for feeling numb. Explore the feeling.

Give yourself permission to cry, to express anger, to be crazy or quiet, to feel a lot or to feel numb. This is your protected sanctuary where you can fully acknowledge the loss of your loved one. Your loved one is dying or has died. Your world has changed both within and without. Cradle yourself in your grief. You need your love, your protection. So be gentle with yourself and take your time. Let yourself be however you are in this moment.

Steps to Develop an Inner Relationship

- Set up a sanctuary to your loved one in a private place in your home. Create an altar with pictures of your loved one and any objects that are meaningful to your relationship. Spend time there regularly: meditate, listen to music, write, cry.
- Before you go to bed, ask for a dream that will guide and heal you in your grief. Put pen and paper by your bed and write down whatever you remember in the morning. When awake, you can reenter a dream and dialogue with your loved one, perhaps asking questions such as these: What do you want? What can I do for you? What do you want to show me? Do you have any messages for me? What do I need to do to develop a relationship with you? Keep a journal of your dreams about your loved one.
- Write a letter to your loved one. Take advantage of the freedoms that the imagination provides: Express yourself without restriction, break old patterns of relating, explore unresolved issues. Write about what you miss, regret, resent, appreciate. Say good-bye, if you never had a chance to do so.
- Write a response from your loved one. As you learn to provide a voice to the other person, you may feel yourself to be simultaneously within yourself and within the other person.
- Write or speak a dialogue. Let the dialogue unfold spontaneously. Don't interfere or control it. Be open to the unexpected, new information, and new ways of relating. You may also speak a dialogue out loud or hear it taking place inside your head.
- Work with guided imagery, such as exercises 6-1, 6-2, and 6-3, "Connecting through Imagery," in chapter 6 (and on pages

223–25). Use all your inner senses to experience the environment you have chosen, and then meet your loved one.

- Be open to the changes in your loved one and in your relation-ship. Don't let old images or memories dictate the relationship as it evolves. Risk seeing and hearing what the imagination sets before you.
- Use internal communication techniques to work through unfinished business and unresolved issues. Speak up; express your repressed feelings. Be honest and authentic. Listen respectfully to the other person. Experiment with stepping inside the other person and experiencing the relationship from their perspective. This practice helps to develop compassion, understanding, and forgiveness.
- Bring the relationship up to the present by communicating to your loved one about the changes that have occurred in your life since his or her death. Share what is important in your life now. Ask for support or guidance.
- Remember that it is never too late to reconcile, to heal old hurts, and to express your love.

Internal Communication with the Dying

Relaxed in your sanctuary, close your eyes, and in your mind's eye visualize entering the room in which the person is dying. Sit down next to the bed. Take a few minutes to experience this room with all your senses. What do you see around you? What can you hear? Are there any smells? Take the person's hand and feel its weight, its temperature, and its texture. With a squeeze of the hand or with your words, let him or her know that you have come to visit. You now have the opportunity to communicate with this person in a way that you never really considered possible before. You can express everything that you want to in order to help resolve conflicts in your relationship.

Picture yourself expressing your love and appreciation as well as your disappointments, regrets, and hurts. Next, in your imagination, listen carefully and respectfully to what your loved one has to say to you. Continue your dialogue until it feels complete. You may then want to spend some time together in silence. When you feel ready to leave, say good-bye and leave the room. Open your eyes and savor your feelings for a few minutes. Then record your experience in the journal reserved for this purpose.

Connecting through Your Heart
with a Dying Loved One

Sit down and close your eyes. For a few minutes, bring your full attention to the pattern of your breathing. Feel the breath passing through your nostrils. Then focus on the heart center on the sternum between your breasts. Be aware of any sensations there, no matter how subtle they may be. You may want to touch that area with your fingers. Once your attention is centered there, breathe in and out of your heart.

Now begin to talk to your loved one through your heart—silently, gently, truthfully, compassionately. Let the words flow through your heart on the waves of your breath. You may want to say that you are fully present, that you care, that you want to support the person in the passage, that you will miss the person when death occurs. Or you might simply send love through your heart. Maintain the physical connection with the heart as you silently speak.

Imagining a Loved One's Passing

In your sanctuary, sit down and close your eyes. Let go of all distractions and concerns and bring your full attention to the internal landscape of your imagination. Imagine that you are sitting beside the person who is dying. What do you see? Smell? Hear? What are you feeling? Be aware of the sound of the person's breathing. Is it smooth or labored? Light or heavy? Synchronize your breathing to his or her breathing so that you are breathing in and out together.

You are participating in a sacred time of transition, sharing the last moments of a life. Now is the time to express your love, whether through words or touch. Are there any unresolved issues you want to bring up? Listen carefully. Does the person want to speak to you? Explore any resistance you feel about letting go of this person, but since letting go may take days, weeks, or months, don't worry about completing this process before going on to the next part of the exercise.

When you are ready, reassure the person that he or she can move on now. Say good-bye. Be fully present and aware of the last breath. This marks the end of a lifetime and the end of your relationship as you have known it. After death has occurred, take time to sit with the body, reflecting on what has just happened and on your loss. Allow yourself to fully experience the impact; cry if you need to. Now that you have participated fully in your loved one's passing, contemplate your own feelings. Notice any subtle changes in the person's body as time passes. You might also become aware of the presence of their spirit in the room.

When you feel ready, prepare to leave. Open your eyes and record what you have experienced.

Seven Steps for Working with Dreams

1. The first step is to establish a relationship with your dreams as messengers from the unconscious. Perhaps you have always ignored your dreams or devalued the messages from this part of your psyche. But most cultures of the world have used dreams as healing tools, and Freud and Jung, the great genius/explorers in the mapping of the human psyche, proved the great value that dreams have for us as conduits to instinct, buried memories, and the unconscious. If you have avoided this area of your reality, you may have to convince the unconscious that you do value its feedback and that now you are willing to listen. If you approach dreams with respect, humility, and receptivity, you will build a constructive relationship with your unconscious.

2. Before you go to sleep, actively decide that you want to remember a dream, that you are open to whatever the unconscious presents to you. If you are currently struggling with a particular problem or issue, ask for a dream that will address it specifically.

Put a pen and paper (or tape recorder) and a flashlight by your bed, and make the commitment to write down whatever fragment or dream that you remember. Then go to sleep. If you awaken in the middle of the night with a dream, write it down immediately. Make brief notes that you can elaborate on later. Many assume that they will remember a dream only to find the next day that it has flown.

In the morning, don't get out of bed or talk to anyone until you have taken some time to reflect on your dreams. Without editing, write down whatever you remember, including fragments. Sometimes a fragment is like the tail of a fish—if you take hold of it firmly, the rest of the dream may follow out of the watery depths. And even if you don't remember the rest of the dream, the fragment itself can often be a rich source of insights.

If you have trouble remembering your dreams, be patient. Don't give up. Some friends and clients have had success with writing on paper or even in the air, "I want to remember a dream tonight." Or you can work with a guided imagery exercise in which you close your eyes, imagine yourself going to sleep and having a dream, and then awakening in the morning with a clear memory of the dream

3. Later, record your dream in a dream journal. Referring to your notes, write the dream in the present tense as though it were unfolding now. Then give it a title. Writing the dream down in a special place gives it importance and sends the message to the unconscious that you are taking its messages seriously.

After you have recorded your dream, take some time to reflect on it. Prepare for the unexpected; admit your ignorance. Approach the dream humbly, setting aside snap judgments. Remember that a dream works on many levels at once; a dream can never be reduced to just one meaning. You may feel baffled, disturbed, and even resistant—all this is natural in working with dreams. Your task at this point is simply to just sit with the dream images and let them work on you. After a lifetime of studying dreams, Carl Jung confessed that they remained a mystery to him. He did not feel confident that his way of working with dreams could be called a method. However, Jung did feel certain that something always came of meditating on a dream, turning it over and over for a period of time.

4. To begin exploring what needs resolution in a dream, ask questions of the dream and of the dream figures. Here are some sample questions to pose to the dream:

- What am I doing or not doing in this dream?
- What are the significant actions in this dream?
- What are the feelings in this dream?
- Who are the dream figures in this dream?
- What are the issues, conflicts, and unresolved situations?

- What possibilities for healing are present?
- What questions does this dream raise for me?
- What images stand out?
- What associations come up for me with each image?
- What is being wounded and/or healed in this dream?
- Does this dream have a relationship to other dreams?
- Do any situations in my daily life come to mind as I reflect on this dream?
- What new choices does this dream suggest or inspire?

Here are some sample questions to ask of the people who appear in your dream:

- What do you want?
- What do you want to show me?
- Do you have any messages for me?
- What is your gift?
- What do I need to do to develop a relationship with you?
- Where do you want to take me?

5. Look for threads connecting this dream with other dreams. If you find yourself dreaming regularly about a similar theme, in your dream journal read carefully over all the dreams in that series. Perhaps an early dream in a series introduces the issues to be explored in subsequent dreams. Or maybe a later dream offers critical information that was missing in earlier ones.

6. As you move through these steps, remember that a dream can never be reduced to just one meaning. If you feel confident about any one interpretation of a dream, stay open to other possibilities as well. Writer/psychologist James Hillman insightfully writes, "If we think back on any dream that has been important to us, as time passes and the more

we reflect on it, the more we discover in it, and the more varied the directions that lead out of it. Whatever certainty it once might have given shifts
into complexities beyond clear formulations each time the dream is
studied anew. The depth of even the simplest image is truly fathomless.
This unending, embracing depth is one way dreams show their love"
(Hillman, p. 200).

    7. Other methods will help you explore your dream further:

- Dialogue with dream figures or images.
- Adopt the persona of the different people, animals, or objects in
  your dream and reexperience the dream from that perspective.
- Paint or draw the dream; sculpt a dream image.
- Act out your dreams.
- In your imagination, go back into the dream and re-dream it. The
  following exercise will show you how to reenter your dream.

Reentering a Dream

When you have a dream about one who has died, write it down. Take a few minutes to recall the most significant or vivid part of the dream in which this person appeared. Then, close your eyes and reenter the dream by placing yourself in that environment. Even if you didn't notice any smells, sounds, or textures in your original dream, experience this place now with all your senses. Look around you. Touch, smell, listen. Continue to explore this environment with your senses until you feel fully present in your body. This will help you move from your memory of the dream to an experience of it in the present.

Next, pay close attention to the person's expression, movements, and dress. If the details seem vague, focus, as you might through the lens of a camera, on one small part of that person. As you concentrate on this part, other details may become clearer. Then expand your focus to include the whole person.

It takes time to develop your inner senses; you may not be able to see images clearly the first few times you work with imagery exercises. Even without gleaning any details of the person, you'll be able to sense his or her presence. Be aware of what you are feeling.

To create an opportunity for interaction, approach the person directly. You may want to ask the questions on page 67 as possible queries of your dream figures.

Questions for Your Letter to a Deceased Loved One

- What experiences have I been through since my loved one's death?
- What do I miss?
- What do I regret?
- What issues in our relationship remain unresolved?
- What do I resent?
- What do I appreciate?
- What have I learned about myself, my loved one, and our relationship?
- What do I want to carry on?

Ask yourself the following questions after you have written your letter:

- Was I open and honest?
- Did I express my love and appreciation?
- Did I address unresolved issues in our relationship?
- Do I still feel regrets?
- Are any resentments still bothering me?
- Is anything left unsaid?
- Do I feel forgiveness? Do I feel more understanding?

Guidelines for Working with Imagery

- Identify who you wish to see, and think about the problems and unresolved issues in your relationship. How have these affected your feelings about this person since the death?
- Set aside a period of uninterrupted time in your sanctuary. Sit down, focusing your attention on your breathing. Let your mind clear and your body settle.
- Close your eyes and, in your imagination, go to a healing place (such as a garden, field, forest, special room, or beach). Explore this environment with all your senses.
- Invite the person to visit you in the place you have chosen for the purpose of healing your relationship. Watch carefully as he or she approaches. Be aware of how you are feeling. You may observe changes in the person; don't hold on to old memories.
- Begin a dialogue, addressing the issues of concern to you. Speak honestly. Don't interfere with what naturally unfolds. You can also just be with this person, sharing the time together in silence.
- Listen carefully and respectfully to the response.
- Be receptive to unexpected developments. For example, the person may take you somewhere or give you something. Someone else may appear.
- Bring your encounter to a close. If you still feel unfinished, tell your family member that you will be soon meeting again in your imagination.
- Spend some time in your sanctuary after the person has departed. Relax and reflect on what has happened.
- Write down what you have experienced. It may take time to understand the meaning or significance of what happened.

Awakening Your Inner Senses

Close your eyes. Let your attention first focus on your breathing. Be aware of the sensations you experience with every inhalation and exhalation. Now imagine yourself standing in the center of a kitchen. There is an open fireplace in one corner. You can hear the crackling of the fire. Move closer and hold up your hands to the fire. Feel the heat. Look closely at the colors in the flames. A pot is simmering on an iron stand in the fireplace, and soup is bubbling over. Smell the aromas. Focus on this, seeing if you can identify what is cooking. You might even be able to smell the herbs flavoring the soup. There is a wooden spoon sitting next to the pot. Pick it up, feeling its texture and weight. Dip it into the pot of soup and scoop out some to taste. Savor it in your mouth, feeling your taste buds responding.

Connecting through Imagery: The Field

Close your eyes. Take a few deep breaths and focus on the movement of each as it flows in and out of your body. Let the breath be your bridge as you shift your attention from the outer world to an inner world of the imagination.

You are standing in a large field that rolls out to the horizon. You see a figure approaching across this field. As the person comes nearer, you realize this is the one you hoped to meet. Be aware of what you are feeling. Notice how this person looks and moves, what he or she is wearing. Has the person changed? Be willing to let go of old pictures; your loved one may look and act in a different way than you remember. Stay in the present with this person, letting your interaction unfold without editing or interfering with what happens.

Let your loved one know how you have felt since the death—what you miss, what you regret, what you appreciate about him or her. Update the person on what has changed for you since the death and take time to listen to all responses and messages. Follow this exchange wherever it may go.

When you feel ready, tell your loved one good-bye. Watch as the person leaves, remaining aware of how you are feeling. Spend some time alone with yourself, reflecting on this experience. Then open your eyes.

Connecting through Imagery: The Rose

Closing your eyes, imagine a rosebud that is still tightly closed. Use all your inner senses to experience this flower: What color is it? How does it feel?

The rose is now beginning to open slowly, petal by petal. At its center stands your loved one, waiting for you. Go to meet the person and allow your interaction to unfold on its own. You may be surprised at what happens between you—some interaction or communication could take place that you never imagined possible in life.

This is a time to update your relationship. Share with this person the changes, feelings, insights and new perspectives you have experienced since the death.

When you are ready, conclude your visit. If you still feel unfinished, let the person know when you will be visiting again. Then step out of the rose's center and watch the petals fold up again, enclosing and protecting the place of your meeting.

Connecting through Imagery: The Star

Close your eyes and imagine yourself sitting on a hill. Above you stretches the night sky with thousands of stars glimmering against a background of black. Thinking of a loved one who has died, let your eyes wander over the entire sky until one star begins to stand out. Looking at this star, observe the threads of light that emanate from its center. One of these threads shines down to where you sit. Follow this beam up to the star. As you move closer and closer, the intense light may blind or overwhelm you. It may take some time for your eyes to adjust.

When you reach the star, step into its center. Your loved one will be waiting for you. Take all the time you need to get reacquainted. Discuss any unfinished business between you; share resentments and regrets as well as appreciations. Then explore your relationship as it is now. Acknowledge the changes, no matter how subtle.

As you prepare to leave, you will be presented with a gift to take back with you. Receive this and descend back to earth on the thread of light.

An Internal Encounter with a Living Family Member

To perform this exercise, sit down, close your eyes, and bring your awareness to your breathing for a few minutes to settle your body and mind. Now imagine a healing place. This can be a place you have seen or visited in ordinary reality, or it may be a place that exists solely in your imagination. Perhaps it exists in nature—a forest, beach, waterfall, mountaintop, garden—or is a special room. You may decide on one particular place only to find that another image presents itself instead. Don't fight this; trust what happens spontaneously.

Experience this place with all your senses. Look around and pay attention to details. Touch, smell, listen. Activating your inner senses is a critical step in this exercise. The more fully attuned you are in your imagination to all your senses, the more intense this experience will be. Continue to explore this environment with your senses until you feel fully present in your body in this place.

When you feel ready, invite the chosen person from your family to join you in this healing environment. As this individual approaches, focus your awareness on any physical sensations you are experiencing. Rather than anticipating what may happen, pay close attention to the person's expression, movements, and dress. Be aware of what you are feeling.

Some people, feeling too anxious to talk with the family member alone even in the imagination, ask for a guide to support and protect them. Standing beside you or behind you, this guide may not actively participate in this encounter but may help you simply by being present.

Begin to address the issues that are of concern to you in your relationship with your family member. Speak honestly and authentically, expressing your feelings fully. This is your opportunity to speak up about the neglected or taboo areas of your relationship.

If you are bringing up an event from the past that you want to resolve, you may want to talk about what happened, how you felt—and feel—about it, how this event affected you, and what you want the person to do about it now. For the best results, avoid blaming, manipulating, or demanding. Still, feel free to express your anger, maintaining your awareness of the sensations in your body. Do this as directly and cleanly as you can. This expression of feeling is for your own healing, not to create a reaction in the other person.

Next, allow your family member to respond. Listen carefully and respectfully. Let the dialogue and interaction unfold spontaneously; don't interfere. You may find that your family member is acting different from ever before. Let this happen. Notice your own resistance to new and unfamiliar ways of relating. You may not understand what is being said. There may be nonverbal communication; there may be silence. Other things may begin to happen. The person—or your guide—may want to show you something. Be receptive to any images that appear. They may seem absurd, disturbing, or confusing, but trust that the imagination is taking you where you need to go for healing. In tapping the imagination, we gain access to a much greater knowledge than our conscious mind can grasp.

For a deeper understanding of your family member's perceptions of and feelings about your relationship, you can step inside that person's body. Look out at the world through his or her eyes. How have you been wounded? How have you struggled in this relationship? What do you want from the person (you, in your own body) standing in front of you? What do you want to say to this person? Allow a dialogue to develop between the *you* within the other person and the *you* relating to that person.

You may find that your meeting begins to move beyond the personal into more soulful concerns. This is not surprising, for the imagination is soul territory and, as Thomas Moore points out, relationships, particularly intensely entangled ones, can lead to the revelation of soul. He writes, "Even though we may think our strong emotions focus on the people around us, we are being set face to face with divinity itself, however we understand or speak about that mystery" (Moore, p. 257).

As your encounter with your family member comes to a close, say good-bye. If you still feel incomplete, let the person know that you will be meeting again in the imagination. Watch your family member leave, being fully aware of all that is going on inside of you. Then spend some time alone in your imaginary healing place reflecting on what has happened and on how you feel now. How have your feelings changed toward this person? Relax and absorb the healing in this place—in your imagination, lie down in the grass, bathe in a waterfall or spring, swim in the ocean, feast on a meal, climb into a warm bed.

Suggestions for Partners

- Remind each other repeatedly that grief creates considerable stress in your partnership/marriage. Escalation of fights and tension are common.
- If you are the nongrieving partner, educate yourself about what your partner is going through: talk to others about grief, read, and listen to tapes to learn whatever you can about the nature and timing of grief. Understand that people grieve in different ways.
- Actively commit to communicate with one another. Set aside specific times to talk, exploring how you are supporting one another, what you need from one another, and how the grief is affecting the relationship. It may be helpful to write one another a Grief Letter (see exercise 8-1).
- If communication has broken down between you or you feel too vulnerable and raw to communicate directly with your partner, consider internal communication techniques, such as the imagery exercises in chapter 6 or the letter-writing activity discussed in chapter 4.
- Take time for yourself without feeling guilty for withdrawing. You need solitary time for reflection and healing. You also may need to take a break from grieving.
- Look at the issues that surface in your marriage—resentments, walls between you, compromises that have become intolerable, unhealthy conditioned responses that go back to your parents' relationship.
- Use grief as an opportunity to be more vulnerable and open with one another. Grief opens hearts.

- Review from time to time the daily losses your relationship has encountered. Have these losses been acknowledged, grieved, and integrated into the marriage? Some losses may need additional healing—perhaps a miscarriage or infidelity. Consider doing a ritual that acknowledges this loss and helps you both let go. You also may want to draw a loss timeline (see chapter 12) to get an overall perspective of the presence of loss in your relationship.
- Acknowledge that grief will change you and your relationship; take time with your partner to identify what you both want in your marriage/partnership.

Writing a Grief Letter to Your Partner/Spouse

Write a letter to your partner, focusing on how grief has affected and changed your partnership. Go into separate rooms and write your letters, being as honest and open as you can. Focus on your feelings and concerns.

If you are the grieving partner, write about your experience of grieving:

- What has been difficult for you?
- What are your fears?
- What have you appreciated about your partner?
- What have you resented or regretted?
- What do you want from your partner?
- Do you feel your partner has supported you?
- If not, what could he or she do to better support you?
- Have any new realizations or understandings come out of your grief?
- What patterns in your relationship do you see more clearly now?
- What changes do you want to make in your relationship?

If you are the nongrieving partner, write about how it has been for you to live with a person who is grieving:

- What has been difficult or challenging for you?
- How have you felt about the changes you've seen in your partner?
- Have you felt left out or abandoned?
- Have you felt appreciated for your efforts to support your partner through this crisis?
- What do you now appreciate, fear, or regret?

· What do you want from your partner?

· What are your visions of the future?

In both cases, write as though your partner were listening with love and understanding. Take the risk of sharing feelings and thoughts that you ordinarily hold back. Try to focus on your own experience rather than blaming or judging your partner.

When you've both finished your letters, exchange them. Take your time to read your partner's letter, reflecting on what has been expressed. You can either write a response or sit down together to talk about your responses.

Suggestions for Parents

- Communicate with your child about death and grief, being as honest and straightforward as your child can understand. Take the time to answer your child's questions, acknowledging what you don't know. Also, remember that children tend to interpret things literally. For example, if you tell him that his grandmother is "sleeping forever" or is "taking a long trip," he might assume that if he goes to sleep he too might sleep forever or that grandmother will return from her trip.

- Take your child's developmental stage into account; you child will not grieve as an adult does. Children do not have the same capacity as adults to tolerate intense pain over a period of time; they will grieve in spurts and may even postpone deep grieving until a later stage of development.

- Share with your child what to expect if she visits a dying family member. If your child doesn't want to go, honor her decision. Explore other ways your child can communicate with that family member—for example, talking through her heart, guided imagery, drawing a picture, or writing a letter.

- Give your child encouragement to grieve and prepare him for what he might experience while grieving—that he might feel sad or unhappy for a while. Invite him to share his feelings and questions with you and help him to express his feelings in ways that are natural and safe for him, utilizing play and the imagination.

- Include your child in funerals and memorials; it is her right to be included. Attempts to protect your child from death and grief can have long-lasting negative effects. However, don't force a child to go to a funeral if she doesn't want to. And honor her

refusal to participate in any part of the ceremony—she
may not, for example, want to look inside the casket or kiss
the dead person.

- Attend to your own grieving. Your modeling of healthy grieving is
more important than you realize. Show your child how you are
taking care of yourself in your grief. Your child might want to help
you create an altar for the sanctuary and, if she sees you using it
regularly, might choose to use that herself from time to time.

Writing a Fairy Tale

Create a stack of index cards with the names of places, animals and other creatures, magical beings, magical objects, and people (see the groupings below for suggestions). Then place these cards face down in stacks, one for each category. Choose a time, such as bedtime, and create an environment that is conducive to storytelling. Ensure that you will not be interrupted. Close the door, light a candle, and gather special toys around the bed. Invite your child to choose one card randomly from each of the five stacks. Reading each one out loud, lay the chosen cards before you both.

Ask your child to start with the magical opening "Once upon a time" and tell you a fairy tale that features these five words. Encourage your child to use the words in any order and to add any other words desired. If your child expresses doubts about being able to create a fairy tale, assure him or her that the fairy tale, once started, will soon begin to tell itself.

An older child may choose to write the fairy tale rather than tell it out loud. Then one of you can read it out loud to the other.

When the fairy tale is finished, ask your child to give it a title. Your child might also illustrate the fairy tale and then create a small book.

Take some time to reflect on your child's fairy tale. What is the central challenge or test in the story? What form does help or guidance take? How does the central character overcome adversity, and how is that character strengthened by these ordeals? Does the fairy tale reflect your child's inner conflicts or anxieties? Does the fairy tale inspire new perspectives and insights? Did you observe any changes in your child after the fairy tale was written? If so, what changes? How can you support any growth or new perspectives that your child's fairy tale inspired?

- *Places*: Mountain, bazaar, sea, valley, pool, lake, desert, castle, mountain pass, village, cave, tunnel, meadow, tree, garden, forest, fire, dungeon, church, bridge, city, crossroads, fountain, hollow, island, palace, river, ship, temple, tower, volcano, wall, door, house, spring
- *Animals and other creatures*: Turtle, raven, worm, serpent, dove, whale, horse, fish, sparrow, crane, camel, lamb, rat, owl, frog, swan, fox, crocodile, dog, cat, swallow, bear, lion, eagle, monkey, bee, pig, dolphin, peacock, ox, hare, lion, cock, wolf, bull, butterfly, crow, dove, elephant, leopard, spider, stag, vulture, hawk
- *Magical beings*: Unicorn, dragon, troll, giant, fairy, goblin, mermaid, angel, sorceress, dwarf, monster, wizard, soothsayer, fairy godmother, phoenix, centaur, griffin, trickster, shaman
- *Magical objects*: Egg, gold, cauldron, ring, ivory, stone, crown, shell, cross, treasure, seed, chalice, drum, star, horn, anchor, pearl, bell, arrow, ladder, sword, rose, book, ax, bone, bow, candle, cloak, crystal, diamond, feather, fire, flute, goblet, chalice, grail, helmet, herbs, jewel, key, lamp, lyre, mask, mirror, pearl, rope, veil, trident, thunderbolt, torch, thorn, moon, sun, thread
- *People*: Harpist, hermit, knight, princess, prince, queen, king, mother, father, grandmother, grandfather, musician, old man, old woman, harlot, wild man, child, clown, farmer, priest, priestess, nun, monk, maiden, carpenter, healer, girl, boy, pirate, gypsy, fool, brother, sister, virgin, twin, invalid, friend, orphan, crone

How You Can Support a Grieving Friend

To better support your grieving friend, remember that using internal communication techniques will help you maintain a connection with your friend even if he or she has withdrawn from you. You can work with imagery to meet your friend in an imaginal world, write a letter, or create a dialogue. These suggestions will also help you integrate grief into your friendship day to day:

- Educate yourself about what your grieving friend is going through. Read books on grief, listen to tapes, talk with others who have grieved. You can expect your grieving friend to be emotional, raw, restless, and unpredictable. Don't expect normalcy too soon. Your friend may want to be with you sometimes and alone at others. He or she may want to talk sometimes and remain silent with you at others. Take your friend's lead.

- It is important to acknowledge the death and the impact it has had on your friend. Recognize that your friend is in an altered state. Understand if you can that moods will shift abruptly and that simple contact can be greatly soothing. Express interest in your friend's feelings and concerns. Remember that you don't have to make your friend feel better. If your friend cries, be as supportive as you can. If your friend needs to talk, listen. Be trustworthy with confidences. Avoid giving lots of advice, even though you may feel impelled to do this because you feel helpless in the face of so much pain.

- Help in small ways. You can bring meals and flowers, offer to do errands, send cards, and check in regularly by phone.

- Be willing to admit your helplessness in the situation and be honest if you feel overwhelmed or frightened by the intensity of your friend's feelings. You may need to pull back for a while. If so, let your friend know that you are doing this.
- Try not to take rejection personally. Many people who are grieving don't have the energy to be considerate or nice.
- Your friendship will probably change throughout your friend's grief. Some friendships deepen, but some drift away. Grieve the loss of the old friendship and be open to changes.

Healing the Grief Passed Down through Generations

Sit down, close your eyes, and focus your awareness on your breathing, breathing into your belly. Relaxing tensions as you exhale, become more and more present to this moment. Notice the feelings and sensations that are occurring now.

Feel your awareness expanding, transcending the limitations of space and time. Your imagination is fluid here, full of possibilities for healing.

Imagine yourself in a peaceful place where you can nourish your spirit—in the mountains, in a forest, by the sea. Create the scenery around you, experiencing its sounds, sights, and smells. Let there be a body of water nearby—perhaps a river, lake, or the ocean. Take some time to relax in this place, absorbing the tranquillity and peace.

Invite your family member to join you here for the purpose of healing the unresolved grief that has been passed down through the generations. Introduce him/her to this place, again taking time to take in the peaceful-ness so that both of you are relaxed and receptive. There is no need to hurry.

Find a comfortable place to sit with your family member. Now invite him/her to share with you the grief that has been held in his heart. You are simply to listen as he gives expression to feelings that may have never been expressed. As you listen, you are able to see with the eyes of the imagination the unresolved grief in his heart. What does it look like? What color is it? What texture? Look into your own heart. Do you see that same unresolved grief hidden there?

When your family member has finished sharing, ask if he or she is ready to let that grief go now. If he is not, let him know that you will be returning on another day to talk and be together for further healing.

If your family member is ready to let go of that grief, invite her to gather that grief, scooping it out of her heart with her hands. Walk with her as she carries that grief to the river, sea, or lake where she will throw it into the water. Watch as that grief dissolves and disappears; it is being cleansed and transformed.

If that unresolved grief has been passed down to you, gently gather it from your heart into your hands—this grief does not belong to you. Carry it to the water and place it in the water where it can be cleansed and transformed. Again, watch it dissolve and disappear. Experience what it feels like to no longer be carrying this grief.

After this is done, just be together with your family member. Feel the peace that is within you—know that peace is within you.

Opening the Heart

Close your eyes and focus on the heart center at your sternum between your breasts, that same point which you focused on in exercise 2-2, "Connecting through Your Heart with a Dying Loved One," in chapter 2. You may want to use your thumb to press gently into that point. Breathe into this point as you push into the sensitivity there. Each breath carries you deeper into your heart. Slowly open to the pain held there, the losses of a lifetime hidden away in the dark corners.

Let your heart experience all the pain of loss—the loss of your parents, of your children, of your dreams, the separation from those you love, the grief of putting yourself out of your own heart. Let your heart open to these losses. Cradle them with compassion. Feel the grief, the ache, the longing—all the tears unshed, the moments unlived. Make room in your heart for the pain and for the healing. Keep breathing into your heart, feeling it grow more spacious. Learn to not close your heart when there is pain.

Bibliography

Achterberg, Jeanne. *Imagery in Healing: Shamanism and Modern Medicine*. Boston: Shambhala, 1985.

Allende, Isabel. *Paula*. New York: HarperCollins, 1994.

Ashley, Judy A. "My Mother's Hair." In *Loss of the Ground-Note: Women Writing about the Loss of Their Mothers*, edited by Helen Vozenilek. Los Angeles: Clothespin Fever Press, 1992.

Bettelheim, Bruno. *The Uses of Enchantment: The Meaning and Importance of Fairy Tales*. New York: Random House, Vintage Books, 1989.

Boa, Fraser. *The Way of the Dream: Conversations on Jungian Dream Interpretation with Marie-Louise Franz*. Boston: Shambhala, 1994.

Bradshaw, John. *Bradshaw On: The Family: A Revolutionary Way of Self-Discovery*. Deerfield Beach, Fla.: Health Communications, 1988.

Bynum, Edward Bruce. *Families and the Interpretation of Dreams: Awakening the Intimate Web*. New York: Harrington Park Press, 1993.

Byrd, Richard. *Alone*. New York: Kaodansha International, 1995.

Callanan, Maggie, and Patricia Kelley. *Final Gifts: Understanding the Special Awareness, Needs, and Communications of the Dying*. New York: Bantam Books, 1993.

Colette. *My Mother's House and Sido*. New York: Ferrar, Straus & Giroux, 1975.

Doore, Gary, ed. *What Survives? Contemporary Explorations of Life after Death*. Los Angeles: Jeremy P. Tarcher, 1990.

Epel, Naomi. *Writers Dreaming: Twenty-Five Writers Talk about Their Dreams and the Creative Process*. New York: Random House, Vintage Books, 1993.

Eppinger, Paul, and Charles Eppinger. *Restless Mind, Quiet Thoughts: A Personal Journal*. Ashland, Ore.: White Cloud Press, 1994.

Garfield, Patricia. *The Dream Messenger*. New York: Simon & Schuster, 1997.

Hillman, James. *The Dream and the Underworld*. New York: HarperCollins, 1979.

Houston, Jean. *The Search for the Beloved*. Los Angeles: Jeremy P. Tarcher, 1987.

Jampolsky, Gerald G. *Forgiveness: The Greatest Healer of All*. Hillsboro, Ore.: Beyond Words Publishing, 1999.

Jung, C. G. *Memories, Dreams, Reflections*. New York: Random House, Vintage Books, 1961.

Kalish, Richard A., and David K. Reynolds. *Death and Ethnicity: A Psychocultural Study*. Los Angeles: University of Southern California Press, 1976.

Kaplan, Louise. *No Voice Is Ever Wholly Lost: An Exploration of Everlasting Attachment between Parent and Child*. New York: Simon & Schuster, 1995.

Kast, Verena. *A Time to Mourn: Growing through the Grief Process*. Einsiedeln, Switzerland: Daimon Verlag, 1988.

Kennedy, Alexandra. *Losing a Parent: Passage to a New Way of Living*. San Francisco: HarperSanFrancisco, 1991.

Kramer, Kenneth P. *The Sacred Art of Dying: How the World Religions Understand Death*. Mahwah, N.J.: Paulist Press, 1988.

Larsen, Stephen. *The Mythic Imagination: The Quest for Meaning through Personal Mythology*. New York: Bantam Books, 1990.

Lerner, Harriet. *The Dance of Intimacy: A Woman's Guide to Courageous Acts of Change in Key Relationships*. New York: HarperCollins, 1989.

———. *The Mother Dance: How Children Change Your Life*. New York: HarperCollins, 1998.

Levine, Stephen. *Who Dies? An Investigation of Conscious Living and Conscious Dying*. Garden City, N.Y.: Doubleday, Anchor Books, 1982.

McLeod, Beth Witrogen. *Caregiving: The Spiritual Journey of Love, Loss and Renewal*. New York: John Wiley and Sons, 1999.

———. "The Caregivers." *The San Francisco Examiner*, April 9, 1995.

Miller, Sukie. *After Death: How People around the World Map the Journey after We Die*. New York: Simon & Schuster, 1997.

Mindell, Arnold. *Coma: Key to Awakening*. Boston: Shambhala, 1989.

Moore, Thomas. *Soul Mates: Honoring the Mysteries of Love and Relationship*. New York: HarperCollins, 1994.

Nietzsche, Friedrich Wilhelm. *The Portable Nietzsche*. Edited by Walter Kaufmann. New York: Viking, 1977.

Nouwen, Henri J. *In Memoriam*. Notre Dame, Ind.: Ave Maria Press, 1980.

O'Donohue, John. *Eternal Echoes*. New York: HarperCollins, 1999.

Rando, Therese A. *How to Go On Living When Someone You Love Dies*. New York: Bantam Books, 1991.

Remen, Rachel Naomi. *My Grandfather's Blessings: Stories of Strength, Refuge and Belonging*. New York: Putnam, Riverhead, 2000.

Rinpoche, Sogyal. *The Tibetan Book of Living and Dying: A New Spiritual Classic from One of the Foremost Interpreters of Tibetan Buddhism to the West*. San Francisco: HarperSanFrancisco, 1992.

Roth, Philip. *Patrimony*. New York: Simon & Schuster, 1991.

Saint-Exupery, Antoine de. *The Little Prince*. New York: Reynal & Hitchcock, 1943.

Satir, Virginia. *The New Peoplemaking*. Mountain View, Calif.: Science and Behavior Books, 1988.

Saunders, Cicely. "I Was Sick and You Visited Me." *Christian Nurse International*, no. 4 (1987).

Savage, Judith A. *Mourning Unlived Lives: A Psychological Study of Childbearing Loss*. Wilmette, Ill.: Chiron Publications, 1989.

Ulanov, Ann, and Barry Ulanov. *The Healing Imagination: The Meeting of Psyche and Soul*. Mahwah, N.J.: Paulist Press, 1991.

Viorst, Judith. *Necessary Losses*. New York: Fireside, 1986.

Von Franz, Marie-Louise. *On Dreams and Death: A Jungian Interpretation*. Boston: Shambhala, 1987.

Watkins, Mary. *Waking Dreams*. Dallas, Tex.: Spring Publications, 1976.

Welshons, John E. *Awakening from Grief: Finding the Road Back to Joy*. Little Falls, N.J.: Open Heart Publications, 2000.

Whyte, David. Workshop: Association of Transpersonal Psychology Annual Conference, Asilomar, Calif., August 4, 1991.

Wickes, Frances G. *The Inner World of Childhood*. Englewood Cliffs, N.J.: Prentice Hall, 1972.

About the Author

Alexandra Kennedy, M.A., is a psychotherapist in private practice in Santa Cruz, California, and author of *Losing a Parent* (HarperSanFrancisco, 1991). She has led workshops and lectured on grieving at universities, hospices, churches, and professional organizations. She is a faculty member at the University of California Santa Cruz Extension. Her articles have appeared in *Yoga Journal*, *Mothering* magazine, and *California Therapist*. She has been interviewed in *New Woman*, *USA Today*, *San Jose Mercury News*, *San Francisco Examiner*, and *Boston Herald* as well as on NPR's "Talk of the Nation," CNN's "Sonja Live," KQED's "Family Talk," and "New Dimensions Radio."

To share responses to *The Infinite Thread: Healing Relationships beyond Loss* or to obtain information regarding workshops and lectures, you may go to the Web site *www.alexandrakennedy.com* or write to

Alexandra Kennedy
P.O. Box 1866
Soquel, CA 95073

OTHER BOOKS FROM
BEYOND WORDS PUBLISHING, INC.

Teach Only Love
The Twelve Principles of Attitudinal Healing
Author: Gerald G. Jampolsky, M.D.
$12.95, softcover

From best-selling author Dr. Gerald Jampolsky comes a revised and expanded version of one of his classic works, based on *A Course in Miracles*. In 1975, Dr. Jampolsky founded the Center for Attitudinal Healing, a place where children and adults with life-threatening illnesses could practice peace of mind as an instrument of spiritual transformation and inner healing—practices that soon evolved into an approach to life with profound benefits for everyone. This book explains the twelve principles developed at the Center, all of which are based on the healing power of love, forgiveness, and oneness. They provide a powerful guide that allows all of us to heal our relationships and bring peace and harmony to every aspect of our lives.

Forgiveness
The Greatest Healer of All
Author: Gerald G. Jampolsky, M.D.; Foreword: Neale Donald Walsch
$12.95, softcover

Forgiveness: The Greatest Healer of All is written in simple, down-to-earth language. It explains why so many of us find it difficult to forgive and why holding on to grievances is really a decision to suffer. The book describes what causes us to be unforgiving and how our minds work to justify this. It goes on to point out the toxic side effects of being unforgiving and the havoc it can play on our bodies and on our lives. But above all, it leads us to the vast benefits of forgiving.

The author shares powerful stories that open our hearts to the miracles which can take place when we truly believe that no one needs to be excluded from our love. Sprinkled throughout the book are Forgiveness Reminders that may be used as daily affirmations supporting a new life free of past grievances.

Every Day God
Heart to Heart with the Divine
Authors: David and Takeko Hose
$14.95, softcover

When Takeko Hose was accidentally shot and paralyzed from the knees down, she and her husband, David, reached out desperately for divine assistance through a succession of what David calls "naked prayers." *Every Day God* is the record of a remarkable communication between authors David and Takeko and God. Not a stickler for ritual, a lofty voice from beyond, or an enigma, their God is a warm and caring parent, eager to nurture and love unconditionally all of His children. Comforting and enlightening, the teachings in *Every Day God* are lighthearted, often humorous, and relevant to modern life. And at the core of each teaching is an invitation to meet this largely undiscovered self within our innermost hearts, a self that flows from our divine source.

The Great Wing
A Parable
Author: Louis A. Tartaglia, M.D.; Foreword: Father Angelo Scolozzi
$14.95, hardcover

The Great Wing transforms the timeless miracle of the migration of a flock of geese into a parable for the modern age. It recounts a young goose's own reluctant but steady transformation from gangly fledgling to Grand Goose and his triumph over the turmoils of his soul and the buffeting of a mighty Atlantic storm. In *The Great Wing*, our potential as individuals is affirmed, as is the power of group prayer, or the "Flock Mind." As we make the journey with this goose and his flock, we rediscover that we, too, tie our own potential into the power of the common good through honesty, hope, courage, trust, perseverance, spirituality, and service. The young goose's trials and tribulations, as well as his triumph, become our own.

Seeing Your Life Through New Eyes
InSights to Freedom from Your Past
Paul Brenner, M.D., Ph.D., and Donna Martin, M.A.
$14.95, softcover

    Seeing Your Life Through New Eyes is in a hands-on workbook format that helps you create a diary of self-discovery and assists you in resolving any misunderstood relationships. You can learn how to uncover unconscious patterns that define how you love, what you value, and what unique gifts you have in life. This book reveals those obstacles that too often interfere with loving relationships and creative expression, and it includes diagrams to use for your personal exploration and growth.

The Intuitive Way
A Guide to Living from Inner Wisdom
Author: Penney Peirce; Foreword: Carol Adrienne
$16.95, softcover

    When intuition is in full bloom, life takes on a magical, effortless quality; your world is suddenly full of synchronicities, creative insights, and abundant knowledge just for the asking. *The Intuitive Way* shows you how to enter that state of perceptual aliveness and integrate it into daily life to achieve greater natural flow through an easy-to-understand, ten-step course. Author Penney Peirce synthesizes teachings from psychology, East-West philosophy, religion, metaphysics, and business. In simple and direct language, Peirce describes the intuitive process as a new way of life and demonstrates many practical applications from speeding decision-making to expanding personal growth. Whether you're just beginning to search for a richer, fuller life experience or are looking for more subtle, sophisticated insights about your spiritual path, *The Intuitive Way* will be your companion as you progress through the stages of intuition development.

To order or to request a catalog, contact

Beyond Words Publishing, Inc.
20827 N.W. Cornell Road, Suite 500
Hillsboro, OR 97124-9808
503-531-8700 or 1-800-284-9673

You can also visit our Web site at *www.beyondword.com*
or e-mail us at *info@beyondword.com*.

BEYOND WORDS PUBLISHING, INC.

OUR CORPORATE MISSION:
Inspire to Integrity

OUR DECLARED VALUES:
We give to all of life as life has given us.
We honor all relationships.
Trust and stewardship are integral to fulfilling dreams.
Collaboration is essential to create miracles.
Creativity and aesthetics nourish the soul.
Unlimited thinking is fundamental.
Living your passion is vital.
Joy and humor open our hearts to growth.
It is important to remind ourselves of love.